ForeX Trading
for
Maximum Profit

ForeX Trading for Maximum Profit

THE BEST KEPT SECRET *OFF* WALL STREET

RAGHEE HORNER

EDITED BY JEFFREY ALAN BRANDZEL

WILEY

JOHN WILEY & SONS, INC.

To my Ma, Nila, and Herbie. You are all my reasons.

For general information about our other products and services, please contact our Customer Care Department within the United States at 800-762-2974, outside the United States at 317-572-3993 or fax 317-572-4002.

Wiley also publishes its books in a variety of electronic formats. Some content that appears in print may not be available in electronic books. For more information about Wiley products, visit our web site at www.wiley.com.

ISBN: 0-471-71032-6

Printed in the United States of America
10 9 8 7 6 5 4 3 2 1

ACKNOWLEDGMENTS

This book has been the culmination of some very hard work from a number of people.

I truly believe there are no coincidences in life. I have been fortunate enough to have truly talented and wonderful people with me throughout this journey. And in no particular order—if you will indulge me—I would like to thank them.

To Dale and Sasson, the fire that kept this project burning! You both are truly unwavering and irreplaceable.

To Jeffrey—without your guidance these pages could not have been written.

To David F., in one conversation you turned my world upside-down…in a wonderful way! You got the ball rolling.

To David W., the master communicator.

To Raphel and Marisa of eSignal, for all your help.

To Chris, the best programmer a girl could want—you make my charts sing.

To my students. You are the inspiration that runs throughout this book. You have impacted my life and trading more than you will ever know. You push me to be better, and for that you all have been the best teacher I could ever have!

To my Ma—everything I do is to make you proud. To my husband Herbie for your unconditional support to follow my dreams. To my sister Nila, for your example of what it means to be dedicated.

ForeX Trading for Maximum Profit

CONTENTS

Introduction

You are reading this book for one simple reason: You want to trade Forex successfully, which is to say you want to be a profitable Forex trader. I'm not going to lose sight of this fact. In fact, I can tell you why I chose to take on the painstaking effort of writing this book.

About four years ago, more than a few of my students wanted to trade Forex and I did not have a book or course to recommend to them. I did visit many bookstores in an effort to find even one book that I felt provided would-be Forex traders a methodology they could follow. My search yielded no results. Let me tell you what I did find. I found books that discussed the history of the Forex, books that discussed the interbank relationship, books that discussed the pairs and fundamentals of the Forex market, and finally books that discussed all the patterns and indicators you could use in the Forex market. I call the last type of book "glossary" books because that's all that they are: a collection of definitions and descriptions with no step-by-step methodology.

I was frustrated. Surely there had to be a book that discussed a proven style of Forex trading that wasn't reliant upon a software system or proprietary approach. That was when I finally decided to start writing, if for no other reason than to share what I had learned after over a decade in the markets. When people ask me about the Forex market I tell them that it has the best features of all the other markets with none of the problems. I still feel this way. What other market can guarantee stops? What other market has zero commissions? (We do pay the spread and I will discuss that in-depth, but consider that you often pay the spread in stocks and futures as well.) What other market has 24-hour liquidity? What other market trades with no gaps Monday through Friday? These are qualities that make for a "dream" market.

I have to admit, maybe there's a bit of vanity, too. I wanted to share my style and my views. I envisioned a dialogue between myself and you the reader. I envisioned that some of my statements might raise an eyebrow and others a smile. I wanted to shatter myths that have propagated in the markets regarding trading. More than anything I wanted to set forth a tried and true formula for trading success; a formula that didn't rely on systems and complex calculations, one that would be as effective for a new trader as for the seasoned trader. Please don't be fooled into thinking that a successful trading approach needs to be complicated. It doesn't. Some of you will have to take my word for it and some of you already know this.

If there is anything that has continued to serve me well as I trade the markets it is my willingness to question. Have you ever wondered why trading types like scalping, momentum, or swing trading, areas defined by how long you are in the trade? That couldn't be further from the truth and we discuss that in Chap. 15, "The Difference Between Scalping, Momentum, Swing, and Position Trading. Ever wonder what "multiple confirmation" is or why it's important? That very question was asked of me during the interview conducted for this book. Ever wonder which economic reports a Forex trader must be on the look out for and how to gauge the market's reaction to their release? We'll talk about that in Chap. 25, "News Discounting." Did you know that most traders learn and use the wrong type risk management for trading? This is exactly what I address in Chap. 20, "Rewriting Trade Management." Would you like to learn how to use the MACD Histogram to confirm momentum trades? I'll cover how I do it in Chap. 22, "Placing Your Orders."

This book is a focused study on the specifics of trading the Forex market. There are plenty of other books that will give you definitions and descriptions. The trading community certainly doesn't need another one from me. I will only discuss the subjects I know inside out and only the strategies that I actually use. When you complete this book you will have learned my personal, step-by-step approach. No detail is hidden. You are "looking over my shoulder" as I explain

how to trade the Forex markets. And I am honored that you are allowing me, if even for a short time, to be your teacher. I have learned from many teachers as I sought to become a successful trader. The ones that always taught me the most were the ones that showed me the market through their eyes and didn't try to be everything to everyone. It's that level of honesty that contributed the best of my education. I'm here to tell you that my style may not be your cup of tea. If you have that level of honesty with yourself you will go far in your efforts to become a trader. However, I do believe that many of you will find that the three-step approach taught in this book is a strategy that is easy to recognize and repeat. No matter how effective a strategy, if it can't be understood and followed, it is useless. I speak from experience. No one is born knowing how to trade; we all must begin the journey somewhere. If that's where you are now—beginning your journey into trading—I envy you. You are now embarking on an exciting journey that will teach you about the markets and about yourself. If you are an experienced trader seeking to learn more about the Forex market, welcome! Together we will be demystifying the foreign exchange and discussing a methodology you will be able to put to work as soon as you finish this book.

Let's begin!

CHAPTER 1

Trading ForeX

Trading ForeX

You may be asking yourself, "Why haven't I heard of this market before now?" If this trading market is relatively new to you, don't feel like you are alone.

Let's explore what every trader or investor needs to know about Forex. The foreign exchange or "Forex" (also called the spot market) is the largest market on the planet. This is an irrefutable fact. Its average $1.5 trillion to $2 trillion traded per day is almost 100 times that of the $25 billion of the NYSE. And while we will be discussing this in depth later, remember, size has its advantages.

The Forex market may seem like a new market to those of us in the United States but in actuality this market has been around for many years. There are two developments that brought Forex trading to life and to the United States. First was the decision that led to the free-floating market we trade today. The catalyst was President Richard M. Nixon's decision to abandon the gold standard in 1973. Subsequently, the fixed-rate system fell apart and currency values were set by supply and demand. Second was the Commodity Futures

Modernization Act of 2000 approved by Congress on December 15, 2000, and signed into law by President William J. Clinton on December 21, 2000.

The Commodity Futures Modernization Act is a significant step forward for U.S. financial markets. This important law creates a flexible structure for regulation of futures trading, codifies an agreement between the Commodity Futures Trading Commission (CFTC) and the Securities and Exchange Commission to repeal the 18-year-old ban on trading single stock futures and provides legal certainty for the over-the-counter derivatives markets.

Before late 1999, Foreign Exchange was largely unknown to the U.S. public because retail Forex brokerages simply did not exist in the numbers they do today nor were they regulated. The Commodity Futures Modernization Act allowed the CFTC (Commodity Futures Trading Commission) to regulate and oversee the Forex Exchange brokerages. Subsequently, most Forex firms became members of the National Futures Association.

We now know that the Foreign Exchange isn't anything new, so why are we hearing so much about it now? As with many things in life and trading, it's all about timing. Once the Commodity Futures Modernization Act was passed, regulated retail brokerages starting popping up. With zero commissions they should have garnered some attention back in 1999–2000, but they didn't. Why? Well let me ask you, do you recall what was going on back in 1999? The U.S. stock market was three solid years into a rally, the likes of which cast a shadow on all other markets! Also a factor was the introduction of two very popular futures contracts. The Chicago Mercantile Exchange (CME) introduced the E-Mini S&P 500 and Nasdaq 100 contracts in September 1997 and June 1999, respectively. Consider that most futures traders were already familiar with well-established currency contracts traded through the CME and didn't know of the alternative. Subsequently, not a lot of people cared that the foreign exchange market was now regulated and retail brokers were ready to take orders online.

As with all cycles, what goes up must go down, and all great traders and investors never stop looking for a market to put their money into. The Foreign Exchange market offers the best trading hours (24-hours a day!), massive liquidity, no commissions, no margin calls, leverage, and no gaps. And if this wasn't enough, most brokerages will guarantee stop-loss orders. The only guaranteed stops I have seen were only in my dreams!

No Gaps and Guaranteed Stops.

There are no gaps in this market and stops are guaranteed. You may be wondering, "Did I read that correctly?" Yes, you did. Because the market doesn't have any gaps, you never have to deal with gap opens. The 24-hour trading and massive liquidity virtually guarantee that your stops will be executed without slippage. Although you should check with your brokerage, most firms offer this guarantee Sunday through Friday. As an experienced stock and futures trader I know better than to ask for that from my futures or stockbroker. The futures and stock markets simply can't offer traders this guarantee mainly because of limited trading hours that result in frequent gap opens.

For those of you who may be new to the concept of "gaps," a gap open occurs when a market opens higher or lower than the last trading session's close resulting in a literal jump or "gap" in prices. Any stop-loss orders priced within this gap will not be executed at the stop-loss price but rather will become market orders at the next available price. Ouch!

24-Hour Accessibility and Liquidity

The Forex market is open 24 hours, six days a week, opening Sunday evening (EST) and closing Friday afternoon. Let's imagine waking up on Tuesday morning. While New York was sleeping, Sydney, Tokyo, Singapore, Hong Kong, Frankfurt, and London were all trading at various times. London is the most active time zone in the Forex and it is five hours ahead of New York. If New York is considered the center of the stock universe, then London is the center of the Forex universe. Since this is truly a global market, as one time zone finishes trading for the day, another is just beginning or already underway. News and short-term fundamentals have very little to no long-term impact because of the 24-hour, worldwide participation. News can be "digested" over time instead of being concentrated into a 7 1/2 hour trading session like the stock market.

There is no physical location where Forex is traded because it is an "interbank exchange" and is traded electronically through a network of banks, phones, and the Internet. Besides being open 24 hours a day, the Forex market is as large as it is because it is not located in a single city or exchange. In this way it differs greatly from the New York Stock Exchange or the Chicago Mercantile Exchange, both of which trade at a central exchange.

Diversify Your Approach and Portfolio.

Investing in stocks, bonds, and real estate are common ways to diversify a portfolio. Unfortunately, most people do not fully realize the benefits of including currencies to a portfolio. Think of currencies like the stock of a country. Currencies offer a market with high leverage and guaranteed stops. It is also a great market to diversify into because with just six U.S. dollar currency pairs to track, it isn't a time-consuming market to analyze.

Scandals, Manipulation, and News.

While I am a chartist (that means I believe that the news is built into the price action), I do acknowledge that reports can and do effect the Forex markets in the short term. Many times these economic events can be the catalyst of, for example, a breakout or pullback. However, because of the size of the Foreign Exchange market, the effects of news and other outside influences are limited, quickly absorbed, and frankly, react in a more logical fashion. Think of it this way: If you had 10 people in a room and wanted to make them react a certain way to an idea or fact, it probably wouldn't be terribly difficult to change the minds of at least half or more. What if you wanted to do the same to 1,000 or 100,000? What about one million people? How effective would or could you be? Well the Forex trades $1.5 trillion to $2 trillion in currency a day, worldwide, 24 hours a day. This size alone makes it very difficult to manipulate. Even the well-documented Bank of Japan intervention had limited effect on the USD/JPY!

Currencies don't have accounting scandals or wayward CEOs. Consider that because the foreign exchange market is open 24 hours a day, each country can react to whatever relevant information is available at that time. This is precisely why the Forexreacts so logically to news and fundamentals. Many times economic and world events have already been factored into the market by the time New York opens. Because the market is continually open, starting in Sydney and moving on to Hong Kong, Tokyo, Singapore, Frankfurt, London, and New York, it allows the news to be digested by each time zone. Moving from one time zone to another "dilutes" any sudden or extreme reaction that is typically found in domestic markets where there is limited trading hours and where reactions are often exaggerated because many of the participants react to news or fundamentals all at one time.

CHAPTER 2

Getting Started

Getting Started

The market is one of the greatest teachers. It reveals itself to all of us each and every day if we are willing to pay attention. Too many times we try to box it, label it, or beat it.

In the end, all we need to do is study and measure it. With that end in mind, this book is predominately about the specific tools and strategies of trading. In fact, I kept a "sticky note" above my computer screen as I wrote reminding me of my goal: Write a book that could make me a trader again if I forgot everything I knew.

I endearingly labeled this endeavor to friends and family members as the "teach myself to trade from scratch if I got amnesia" book.

If you've been at this trading game for any length of time, you have undoubtedly bought many books. From my experience, most are what I have come to call "glossary education" books. These are those books that include a few paragraphs to a few pages on every conceivable pattern and indicator available, but no real methodology. It's full of definitions and explanations, but when you're through reading it you're no closer to a step-by-step methodology than you were

before reading the book. It's the difference between general information and applicable knowledge.

And just in case I haven't made it abundantly clear, we're here seeking knowledge, my friends.

When I was first getting into trading I didn't know where to start. I had various mutual fund accounts and shares of IBM stock, which I wanted to trade using market timing. Mind you this was years before the Internet as we know it now. I would call my broker or look up quotes in the daily paper and plot the close by hand on my father's old engineering graph paper. Eventually I started trading commodities and I bought a subscription to a service that would mail me charts once a week that I could update by hand until the next set of charts were mailed to my home the following week.

As with many traders who become bored with end-of-day trading, I soon started active trading—"daytrading"—

and sought out intraday charts. So I ordered a service that delivered quotes and charts via satellite. One thing became clear in a hurry: high-tech tools weren't going to make me a trader; having a methodology was going to be the key.

My number-one problem was that I didn't have a methodology. Books on the subject of trading were not nearly as readily available as they are today. So I did the next best thing, I made phone calls to people that I thought could tell me how to get started. I was 17 years old and decided I would phone the people on my list of traders and make a donation to their favorite charity in their name if they would talk with me because I figured they wouldn't talk with a "kid" who was calling out of the blue. Funny enough, I think between my youth and unusual offer, everyone on my list took my call, most by appointment. They were generous with their time, many spending an hour or more answering questions. This time was invaluable but not for the reasons you would think, though.

None of them revealed some closely held secret to trading. (Matter of fact, in hindsight, many of them were actually portfolio managers and investors rather then traders, but it didn't matter.) They all shared one common while dispensing their advice: trade and risk management.

Each of them, all in their own unique way, explained it wasn't so much how you got in the trade, but how you managed it that mattered. When discussing trade or risk management, they all had a set of steps they'd go through, beginning with a matrix of questions they'd asked themselves as they analyzed their positions. From these professionals, I learned the power of asking the right kind of questions when in a trade. Their time was invaluable to me and I am forever grateful to them. And whenever I have a chance to share my experience—successes and failures—I do what those people were gracious enough to do for me: offer my time generously.

After reviewing my notes from those conversations, I knew I needed a blueprint. A blueprint would allow me to "build a trade" the same way over and over again. It would allow me to use a set of tools in a consistent manner. I began to visualize myself as a "trading carpenter." My next problem was that after reading all the glossary books I could get my hands on, I was no closer to finding a set of specific tools that would answer the three questions all traders must ask themselves:

1. **Where to enter the market?**
2. **Where to set my profit targets?**
3. **Where to set my stop-loss?**

This book is dedicated to answering the above questions. It is important to know pertinent facts about the market you are trading, but if the information doesn't answer the three questions just mentioned, it is not helpful or necessary information. In my opinion, traders shouldn't concern themselves with much more than price action. **A chartist or technical trader believes that news is built into price action.** And it is with this philosophy that a chartist or technical trader can participate in any market as long as it is liquid. (A **liquid** market is a market that has enough volume to enter and exit quickly and without significant slippage.)

After reading this book, you will have learned a three-step formula to enter and exit the market, intraday and end-of-day. You will have a set of tools to consistently answer the three questions all traders must ask themselves. Most importantly, you will have a time-tested methodology using classic charting tools from which you can trade the Forex markets! *And let me share a little "secret" with you...I trade all markets this way: stocks, futures, and Forex!*

CHAPTER 3

History Repeats Itself

The Five Mistakes Traders and Investors Make

HISTORY REPEATS ITSELF: The Five Mistakes Traders and Investors Make

There are a number of different methods traders and investors have used to make money in the market. Ranging from fundamentals to technicals, tape reading to charting, the methods to success are as varied as the participants in the markets.

But we all tend to make the same dumb mistakes when we lose money. We're going to discuss the top five because without exception these mistakes are repeated over and over again like a skipping record we won't stop playing. So let's try and stop that cycle right here, right now.

Mistake #1: Trying to Pick Tops and Bottoms

I know what a rush it is to pick a top or bottom successfully. But if the goal of trading is to make money, then the adrenaline rush must be left to our more adventurous pursuits like skydiving and motorcycles. Trading against the trend is a high-risk approach. There are tools that I will teach you to use so that you know exactly where you are within the context of the trend. Even better, you will know

when the market is directionless. Don't try to pick tops and bottoms in the market. Go learn to ride a motorcycle instead. It's more fun and less risky for your wallet.

Mistake #2: Not Selling a Losing Position

Have you heard these words before? "I can't get out now, I'm losing too much." Unrealized losses are still losses. Some losses are only temporary and within the parameters of the stop-loss, traders call it **heat**. Only you can decide what sort of heat you will take. The trades you choose to take will be based upon that tolerance. As traders we must distinguish between heat and losses that are losing trades that we refuse we accept, even when they have broken our stop-loss level. Before entering any trade, you should know at exactly what price the trade becomes "valid"—this is your entry price. We should also know at what price the trade would become "invalid," and this is the level we love to move around: our stop-loss. Solid trade management is the only way to control the tendency of not adhering to your original stop-loss.

We must begin by defining price levels on the chart; we call these **decision levels**. At decisions levels we look to our trade management rules and put our thinking caps on. If we do not predefine decision levels we will be tempted to take action when it is not warranted. Decision levels allow us to time our actions for the right moment. More important, it also allows us to relax until that time that we need to make a decision. This is an important aspect of trading. We can't be focused all day, continuously. We'd burn out! Decision levels allow us to focus our attention to only those times where prices are alerting us potential entries and exits. This reminds me of something I once read about golfer, Tiger Woods. He was explaining how he manages his time and focus:

> My dad has always been a big believer in smelling the roses. I didn't understand that till I got older. It was his way of saying "Don't focus on the task too long or you'll burn yourself out." It was a great lesson, and it was also his way of saying the only real focus you should have is when you're getting ready to play the shot. Talk to your caddie; b.s.; talk to the crowd; look at other things. The game of golf is very beautiful; enjoy it.

I am going off on a slight tangent here, but it is something worthy of discussing as it gives us insight into how we handle the risks and rewards of trading. While I do not like to make comparisons between gambling and trading, there is one comparison that I think speaks volumes about the challenges a trader faces that a gambler does not. If we were to place a bet on a football game, we would do so before the game and then sit back and see what our choice brings. We can't change our bet at halftime or the fourth quarter. A football game has a start and finish. Conversely, a trade is a totally separate event. While the market has a definite open and close, a trade does not. We can change our mind, move our stop, and add to a winning or losing position. It's an event that has no beginning or end, unlike the football game. Because of this, trading poses completely different risk management issues and requires a discipline level that events with a definite beginning and end do not.

Mistake #3: Getting Emotionally Involved in a Trade

This is the reason we don't sell a losing position. We take losses personally, we let our egos get involved, and we hate admitting that we are wrong. We tend to internalize market losses. Realizing a loss is a difficult step, there are five stages that are involved in accepting a loss, and we discuss each stage later in this book.

Mistake #4: Not Making Your Own Decisions

It's easy to be swayed by the news, CNBC, chat rooms, forums, etc. We begin to question our position or worse, we enter a trade based upon other people's opinions. The truth is it is a symptom of a much larger problem: not trusting your methodology. Rule #1 is that no one cares more about your money than you do. When we lack confidence, we give our decision power away hoping that someone or something else can help us. It's easy to understand why we tend to question ourselves. The same curious mind that wants to learn and got us into the market is the same mind that betrays us. Since there are always more indica-

tors and strategies we're begin bombarded with on a daily basis, we wonder "Could that work better than what I have?" And off we go, buying new books, courses, software, and seminars. I've been there, too. I've got boxes full of courses and bookshelves staked with books to show for it.

I would be kidding you if I told you that I don't get curious about these things too! I attend seminars and enjoy them immensely. I read trading books from cover to cover. I get out and meet other traders. This is all because I now have the confidence to sit and listen to others without supplanting what has worked so well for me. I don't have to change my methodology, but I can add new distinctions from what I learn from other traders. It wasn't always this way... there was a time that I was easily swayed or would think I "needed" (more accurately, I "wanted") a particular piece of software or needed to change my style. My husband and I have a saying: "Need" is a funny word. What we think we need is typically what we really just want.

I remember many, many years ago when I was trading with a gentleman who wanted to use a mechanical system to trade about 40–50 stocks. He had been using a trend following system and it had been somewhat profitable for him.

This software was about $5,000.00 and enjoyed immense popularity in the late 90's...you know, when the market went straight up and (literally) chimpanzees were winning stock picking contests. He hired me to execute the trades since I was particularly good at order entry. And I have to admit the curiosity got to me... did this man know something I didn't? Could I be more profitable if I was a systems trader? I had never been a systems trader, and he was convinced he could make me one since I already knew so much about discretionary trading. For a couple weeks we did unbelievably well. I recall we were up about $90,000 midway through the first month. Of course, the voice of reason in my head was screaming, "You're doing well because the market is trending, dummy!"

So I went back to my partner and told him what I thought: *"We'll give back our profits when this market enters a trading range because this [trend following system] will whipsaw us by buying highs and selling lows in a chop. We'll notice when the market enters a trading range but the system won't... to it everything is a trend and it will continue to trade that way."* It fell on deaf ears, because by then this gentleman had calculated projections of what we would make if we continued at the pace we were going...forgetting that the market tends

to chop about the same amount of time that it tends to trend. I don't think I lasted 30 days with my system trading partner, in fact I can't remember at all how we ended it. But I am eternally grateful for the lesson he inadvertently taught me. It wasn't that systems trading doesn't work—it does for some people—just not for me. He taught me what some fish find out too late: Every shiny, flashy object isn't a meal, sometimes it's a lure and that hook may land you in the frying pan.

So I returned to my home office and to the tools I understood well, tools that were well tested, and that I could use in a step-by-step manner day in and day out. I would not follow a "system" but rather become systematic. Doing this would allow me to follow a blueprint and "build a trade" in a consistent manner. To this day, any tools that I use must be able to answer the only three questions that are relevant in trading:

Where should I enter a market?
Where should I place my stop-loss?
Where should I place my profit targets?

Mistake #5: Putting All Your Eggs in One Basket

Diversifying is important for many reasons that you are probably already familiar with. Is it important to make sure that your portfolio is ready for good times and bad, of course, and this means that a portfolio must be diversified into separate markets altogether. What I feel diversification does for a trader is this: It allows us to pick the best trade. If traders only watch a single market, they will tend to try to chase a trade or squeeze more out of a move than may really be there. If traders have alternatives, then they can sit back and let a trade come to them; they can wait for the best possible set up. This is what diversification does for a trader.

I was an avid S&P E-Mini trader for a couple years; in fact, there was a short time when that was all I traded. What a mistake that was! In a nutshell, I traded a high/low breakout method, and I found myself getting frustrated with the lack of breakouts and then a lack of follow-through if the market did manage to breakout. Because I wasn't looking at much else, I would begin to squeeze more out of a trade than it truly merited. Luckily, I snapped myself out of that fairly quickly without too much damage done. You know how sometimes your leg or arm falls asleep? Well my head feel asleep! The experience reminded me to not be lazy—to keep my pulse on the markets—so that when one market flat lines, I can transition to another. There are six major pairs that I will teach you to trade, and with six different markets to track you won't have to chase a trade, you can let the trade come to you. And remember, to diversify means that we add something new to our approach or portfolio, not replace something else that is working.

CHAPTER 4

The Major Players

The Major Players

Many people know the name George Soros as he is synonymous with currency trading. His legendary British pound trade that "broke the bank of England" is well documented.

But what if I told you that a major bank has made over $500 million trading Forex in a single year or that Warren Buffett has invested over $10 billion in currencies? What if I said to you that companies like Coca-Cola, Merck, Dell, Intel, Toyota, and Dow Chemicals all speculate in the Forex market?

Major banks and corporations trade the Forex. Many of the reasons for the size and liquidity of the Forex are the banks and corporations that participate in this market. This is not a new market, however, it is new to individual traders and investors in the United States. To a large degree, because of the Commodity Futures Modernization Act we now enjoy access to this Forex market. For years, though, banks and corporations

have "secretly" participated and profited from this market. A few of the banks that are actively providing market liquidity are Credit Suisse, Bank of America, Goldman Sachs, and Morgan Stanley. Maybe you've heard of them. Corporations take participation in this market very seriously as many have in-house trading divisions or subsidiaries to handle their Forex trading.

Consider that only just over 5% of the activity is generated by companies and governments that do business in a foreign country and convert one currency to another to buy and sell goods and services. So what of the other 90-plus percent? Purely speculation! Because of its sheer size, there is little chance of market manipulation and a single institution dominating the Forex market. *It is for this very reason that the Forex markets adhere so well to charting and technical analysis!*

Even though there is no single dominating entity in the Forex market, there are some major players in this market, so let's discuss who they are. The Major Central Banks are responsible for monetary policy. The Federal Reserve, or the Fed is the central bank of the United States. The Bank of Canada or the BOC is the central bank of Canada and sets Canadian monetary policy. The ECB, or European Central Bank, is responsible for the monetary policy of countries in the European Monetary Union, or EMU. The Bank of England (BOE), the central bank of the United Kingdom, has total independence in setting monetary policy and its nine-member Monetary Policy Committee makes all decisions on interest rates. The Swiss National Bank or SNB, the central bank of Switzerland, is independent in setting exchange and monetary policy. The BOJ or Bank of Japan, is responsible for setting monetary policy in Japan. However, Japan's Ministry of Finance (MOF) controls all foreign exchange policy and therefore is still considered the most important monetary policymaker in Japan. Both the SNB

and BOJ will affect their respective currencies by making remarks and intervening to enforce policy. Because Switzerland and Japan are export-driven countries, there is a preference for a weaker national currency.

Corporations have become increasingly more interested in the foreign exchange. The main cause is the rapid globalization of world economies. A multinational corporation often needs to make payment to another country, which means that many times they must exchange their "home" (or national) currency to that of the country they must pay. In doing so, they are now exposed to depreciation of they national currency. Therefore these corporations have become major players in foreign currency, as they must offset the risk of exchanging national currency for foreign currency. They must hedge against currency depreciation, which will put them on safer financial ground when they make future payments. But corporations do not limit themselves to simply hedging against currency depreciation. The number of corporations speculating in the Forex markets has increased, and with their activity and buying power, they have a continuing impact. However, because the nature of their trading or speculation involves primarily hedging, they tend to take a longer-term approach.

If there is anything I want to impress upon you, it is this: The Forex is a heavily participated market for good reason. Many of the banks and corporations I mentioned earlier are actually making net profits from their speculation. Banks and corporations have had this "playground" to themselves for a long time. I want to encourage you to see why this has been the best kept secret *off* Wall Street.

CHAPTER 5

Prime Trading Times

Prime Trading Times

There are so many aspects of Forex trading that I find appealing: liquidity, leverage, strong trends, no commissions, only six pairs to have to track versus over two dozen commodity futures contracts and 40,000 stocks, no gaps, guaranteed stop-losses... but my favorite aspect of this market is that it is open 24 hours a day, six days a week.

It's said that *the foreign exchange follows the sun around the world* because as one country is closing for the day, another is just opening up.

During the stock market boom, many people didn't have the luxury of watching the market during the day, so active trading was typically ruled out. On the east coast, most folks were already at work before the market opened and returned home well after the market closed. The Forex market is different, it opens Sunday evening and closes Friday afternoon. It trades 24 hours a day with excellent liquidity. What does **liquidity** mean to a trader? It means that there is enough trading volume to assure that you will be able to get into a trade when you want to, but more importantly, you will be able to get out of a trade when you need to! This means that just about anyone can find a time that they can dedicate to Forex trading.

But what times are best? Even though Forex can be traded 24 hours a day, there are some times that are more liquid and better suited to particular currency pairs. The United Kingdom is the most active foreign exchange center followed by the United States, Japan, Singapore, China, Switzerland, Germany, France, and Canada.

Let's discuss the top three foreign exchange centers: The United Kingdom, Japan, and the United States. Together these three centers account for almost 70% of total foreign exchange transactions. London trades, from 3 AM Eastern Standard Time (EST) to 11 AM. London is five hours ahead of New York. Since London is responsible for over 30% of all Forex transactions, most of the large market participants trade during these hours. Since most major reports in the United States are released between 8 AM and 10 AM EST, this overlaps with the already active trading in London and affords some excellent opportunities for those of us on the "other side of the pond." The most active pairs during London trading hours are the EUR/USD, JPY/USD, and the GBP/USD.

Between the hours of 8 AM and 5 PM EST, New York accounts for about 15% to 17% of Forex transactions. The U.S. market is active until about noon EST after which the volume will drop almost in half, due to London's close. This brings up an important aspect of foreign exchange: **market overlap**. The most active market overlap is the New York morning session and the U.K. afternoon. Keep in mind that home or national currency moves in sympathy with the equity markets of that nation, so the U.S. dollar will typically move with the equity markets.

Tokyo, despite it's diminishing role as an active foreign exchange center, still holds one important distinction: It's the first major market to open. Only about 10% of Forex transactions take place between Tokyo's trading hours from 7 PM to 3 AM EST. However, many market participants will use this time to get a pulse of the trading day and begin scaling into positions. The most active pairs are the JPY/USD and AUD/USD.

Fear and greed rule the markets so emotion creates motion, and by knowing when the different pairs are most active we can gain an edge by knowing when specific markets are most likely to be on the move. However, if you are not a night owl or an early riser, have no fear. The majors all rely on the U.S. dollar in part to value the pair so when the U.S. market is open the U.S. dollar and the equities markets will move one another so there are plenty of trading opportunities for those of us who like our beauty rest.

CHAPTER 6

Reading ForeX Quotes

Reading ForeX Quotes

When trading Forex, it is important to understand the price quotes. It may seem daunting at first, but I assure you it's easy to understand once you know what you are looking at.

First things first, the quotes are always presented in pairs. For example: the USD/CAD. This is the U.S. dollar versus Canadian dollar. Since the U.S. dollar is the first currency quoted in the pair it is known as the **base currency** and therefore has a value of 1. In other words *1* USD is equal to *x* CAD. If the current quote for the USD/CAD was 1.3910, that would mean that one U.S. dollar is worth 1.3910 Canadian dollars. Imagine flying to Canada, arriving at the airport and exchanging U.S. dollars for Canadian dollars. This would be a common example of the exchange rate.

There are six major currency pairs to watch. The U.S. dollar versus Japanese yen, U.S. dollar versus Swiss franc, U.S. dollar versus Canadian dollar, euro versus U.S. dollar, British pound versus U.S. dollar, Australian dollar versus U.S. dollar. The order in which the currency pairs

are quoted is not interchangeable: They are fixed. These six pairs are called the "majors." The majors make up almost 90% of daily trading activity.

The first three—the USD/JPY, USD/CHF, and the USD/CAD—all have the U.S. dollar as the base currency and are quoted like the Canadian Dollar example above. The last three—the EUR/USD, GBP/USD, and the AUD/USD—all have the U.S. dollar as the second currency and are quoted differently. Since the first currency quoted in the pair is called the base currency, the second currency quoted in the pair is often referred to as the "second currency" or the "counter currency." When the U.S. dollar is the second currency in the pair, the quote is presented as *1* base currency equals *x* U.S. dollar. So in an example where the EUR/USD quote is 1.1858, *1* euro is worth 1.1858 U.S. dollars. Let's return to the airport scenario. If you flew into a EMU (European Economic and Monetary Union) participating country like Spain and presented your U.S. dollars in exchange for euros, using the example of the EUR/USD quote at 1.1858, you would have to give 1.1858 in U.S. dollars for each euro.

Now I'm not one to get bogged down in facts and history but I find it helpful to know which countries adopted the euro. Twelve of the countries in the EMU adopted the euro (EUR). Those twelve are (in alphabetical order) Austria, Belgium, Finland, France, Germany, Greece, Ireland, Italy, Luxembourg, the Netherlands, Portugal, and Spain. Vatican City also adopted the euro. The euro is not to be confused with the ECU or European Currency Unit, which was actually a theoretical basket of currencies and not an actual currency as bank notes and coins never existed. The euro replaced the ECU concept.

It is when we turn to the charts that we can begin to visualize what the rates mean in terms of the trend. Let's return to the EUR/USD example. When this chart trends upward, it actually means that the euro is strengthening and the U.S. dollar is weakening. In other words, it takes more U.S. dollars to equal one euro. The same is true for the GBP/USD and AUD/USD.

When the U.S. dollar is the base currency (the first currency quoted in the pair) and the chart is in an uptrend, the U.S. dollar is strengthening and the Canadian dollar, Swiss franc, or Japanese yen is weakening. So in the example of the USD/CAD chart, if it is trending up, the U.S. dollar is strengthening and the Canadian dollar is weakening. If the chart is trending down, the U.S. dollar is weakening and the Canadian dollar is strengthening.

A **pip** (price interest point) is like a tick in the stock or futures market. It is the smallest increment of point movement. How do you find out which decimal place in the quote is the pip? Look at the number furthest to the right in the quote; typically it is the fourth decimal place. For example, in a EUR/USD quote of 1.1847, the 7 represents the decimal place that is the pip. So a price movement from 1.1847 to 1.1848 would be a one pip move. All the majors, with the exception of the USD/JPY, have four decimal places and the pip is the fourth decimal place. With the USD/JPY (U.S. dollar vs. Japanese yen), there are only two decimal places, and the second decimal place is the pip.

The pip dollar value is different for some majors. The dollar value for each pip in the EUR/USD, GBP/USD, and AUD/USD is a fixed $10.00. For the CAD/USD, CHF/USD, and JPY/USD, it is not fixed, but rather fluctuates between $7 and $8.

What It Means to Trade in "Pairs"

Frankly, when I first began trading Forex it didn't really matter to me what "pairs" were. I had my charts and simply followed the trends and retracements, and that served me very well. It was just like when I was trading stocks back in the Internet heyday. It didn't matter much to me what the companies did just as long as there was good volume and a reasonable bid/ask spread.

It didn't take very long for Forex to become a larger part of my daily activity and I thought it prudent to learn more about these pairs and the relationship between the two currencies that made the pairs. Since I traded only the "major" or the U.S. dollar pairs, I knew I would have to watch a total of six pairs: the EUR/USD, USD/JPY, GBP/USD, USD/CHF, USD/CAD, and USD/AUD. The reason Forex is traded in pairs is because we are trading the exchange rate between two currencies. An **exchange rate** is the value of one currency against another.

Let's take the EUR/USD, for example. The EUR is the base currency, and the USD is the second or counter currency. If I am buying the EUR/USD pair, exchange rate tells me how much I have to pay in U.S. dollars to buy one euro. If the current quote on the EUR/USD is 1.2300, I would have to pay 1.23 U.S. dollars for one euro. If the U.S. dollar is the base currency, as in the USD/CAD, the exchange rate tells me how much I have to pay in Canadian dollars to buy one U.S. dollar.

When we are trading, we should think of the base currency as the main unit of your buy or sell. So if I were to buy the EUR/USD, I am simultaneously buying the euro (the base currency in this pair) and selling the U.S. dollar (the second currency). When I buy that pair I believe the euro will increase in value versus the U.S. dollar.

If I were to sell the EUR/USD, I am simultaneously selling the euro and buying the U.S. dollar, which means that I believe that the U.S. dollar will increase in value versus the euro. So now I hope you understand what it means to trade in pairs.

CHAPTER 7

Tools of the Trading Game

Tools of the Trading Game

There are two decisions that I credit my trading success to. I've found that the decisions we make early on in any endeavor shape the final outcome.

For some fortunate reason, I decided early on when I was designing my blueprint that I would only use "objective tools" that could project specific price levels on the chart that would serve as entry and exit points. Objective tools are not subject to artful interpretation. A trendline is broken or it is not; an indicator is either showing strength, weakness, or it's neutral. I also decided that I wanted my entries and exits to be established well before I entered the trade, and I wanted these points to be relevant to the price chart and not some set number of points or percentage. Deciding valid risk and reward ratios based upon the price chart was the most important idea that I built into my blueprint. Think about it... *does the market really care that I have set a two-point stop-loss or that I only want to risk 3% on a trade? Does it matter if I want to make $400 on the trade?* Do these arbitrary numbers have any bearing at all on price action or on support and resist-

ance levels on the price chart? You and I both know it does not.

Support and resistance are the most powerful tools I use to decide my entry and exit levels. There are many types of support and resistance: uptrends, downtrends, psychological price levels (or round numbers), moving averages, and Fibonacci Levels. Even though this book is about trading Forex, these tools and blueprint will work on any market or timeframe. And this is due to the nature of the tools: they are universal and robust. Which is simply "system-speak" for the fact that they will work well all on any market and they work consistently. Here's another piece of advice: Be wary of any trading system or tool that only works on specific markets or a specific timeframe. As long as a market is liquid, the tools I am describing will work for you.

Another point worth mentioning was a conscious decision on my part not to rely on indicators for entries and exits. Indicators are to be used as confirmation tools. Since my setups rely on price and chart patterns, it's as easy as glancing at the indicator and taking a quick read on whether it confirms what my price or chart pattern set up is showing. Remember, indicators are all calculated by some combination of adding, subtracting, multiplying, and dividing the market's open, high, low, and close. Because of this, indicators will always lag price action. Indicators can be very helpful, though. I use what I have come to call "on/off indicators," as I only want to use indicators that clearly show buy, sell, or hold without having to determine whether a specific hook or cross has been made.

An on/off indicator can be simply defined as any indicator in which you can take a reading that tells you to buy, sell, or hold. It is does not require that you recognize some sort of hook, cross, pattern, count bars, or any other nonsense that I have seen. You should be able to define an on/off indicator by telling

someone who knows nothing about trading that prices are either—*for example*—trading above or below a Moving Average or that the CCI (Commodity Channel Index) is plotting below the –100 or above the +100 level or that a MACD histogram is above or below the zero or signal line.

Keeping it simple with support and resistance, Fibonacci Levels, moving averages and on/off indicators in hand, I set out to build my step-by-step blueprint. The goal of trading is to find a methodology that will put you in the trade at the right time and more important, take you out of the trade at the right time. Even with that said, if the methodology is not easy to recognize, react to, and repeatable, it doesn't matter how good it is. The tools must be applicable! Furthermore, if you don't understand why and how I use the tools, it won't much matter because throughout this book my goal is to give you the confidence that you can trade successfully with these tools. So let's begin by discussing each tool in detail.

CHAPTER 8

How to Draw Trendlines

How to Draw Trendlines

You've undoubtedly heard of markets that are in an uptrend or downtrend, and we understand that this is a description of the general direction of the market.

But how do we measure it? *We use trendlines.* Trendlines let us know the direction of the trend, the strength of the trend, and also when that trend may break.

Personally, I love trendlines. I spent a lot of years trying to become a "sophisticated" trader. As you get a better at your career you develop a higher, and often, more complicated level of skills. Right? Well, I learned how wrong that could be. In my effort to become a "better" trader all I did was complicate a relatively straightforward endeavor: locate the trend, measure the strength of the trend, project the potential reversals within the trend. So I abandoned my "sophistication" and returned to the tools that I first learned to use when I began teaching myself how to trade. Sometimes we search too hard for answers that are right in front of us.

Grab a ruler, connect at least two swing lows or swing highs on your chart, and what you have is a trendline! We mark trendlines by drawing a straight line connecting the swings or pivots of the market, much like "connect the dot." A **swing (or pivot)** is a previous high or low where the market reverses. They are the peaks and valleys that can be seen on a chart (Ch 8.1). *And by the way, the three lines you see moving in unison across the chart is called the Wave. You'll learn about this tool in Chapter 11, Visual Tools.*

An **uptrend line** is a straight line that is drawn connecting the valleys or swing lows of a market that is rising. We need at least two swings to connect. The swing lows are also considered support levels. **Support** is best described as a "floor." It's an area where prices stabilize and then move up from. Buyers represent support or the "floor." When buyers feel prices are a value or under-priced, they step in and buy and therefore support the market. Support can be both a diagonal line as in an uptrend or a horizontal level.

There are at least two swing lows that were connected to draw this horizontal support level (Ch 8.2). I draw my trendlines from previous swing highs or swing lows then extend these straight lines beyond the current candle or bar. This allows me to project where support or resistance may develop in the future.

Notice that there is more than one uptrend line drawn on the chart (Ch 8.3). In this case we can see there are three: two minor uptrends and one major uptrend. (The major line is designated by the thicker line width) There can be more than one set of trendlines on a chart since support and resistance can develop at more than one level. Frequently we will see both uptrends and downtrends on a chart and this occurrence will typically happen when the market is trading in a range or consolidating.

A word about trendlines: Notice that the

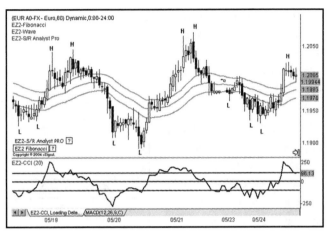

Chart 8.1

major trendlines on the chart have two points that were connected to form the line. These two points are almost four days apart on this 60-minute chart. The two minor trendlines have points that

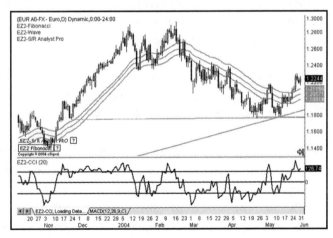

Chart 8.2

are less than a half-day apart. One of the questions that commonly comes up when drawing trendlines, support, and resistance, is how far to look back when choosing swing highs and swings lows to connect, referred to as the look back. The **look back** is how many trading days, candles, or bars we will go back in order to find these swings. I will

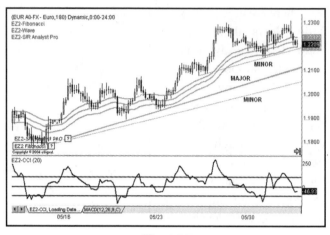

Chart 8.3

typically use a look back of one month to two weeks for intraday charts and one year for end-of-day charts. We know we need a minimum of two swings or "touchpoints" to connect. We use the 30-minute, 60-minute, 180-minute, 240-minute, and the daily charts for our trading and this translates into the following lookback:

- The daily is the easiest to calculate because it means we are going back one year, or approximately 240 trading days.
- The 240-minute chart goes back one month, or 20 trading days, which equals 120 lookback candles or bars.
- The 180-minute chart goes back 20 trading days, which equals 160 lookback candles or bars

- The 60-minute chart goes back two weeks, or 10 trading days which equals 240 lookback candles or bars
- The 30 minute chart goes back 10 trading days, which equals 480 lookback candles or bars

These are just guidelines that allow us to not get caught up in going too far back or using price action that is too recent. For long-term timeframes like the daily or end-of-day chart, the market's memory is about one year. For intermediate term timeframes like the 240-and 180-minute charts, it is 20 trading days or one month. For short term timeframes like the 60- and 30-minute charts, it is 10 trading days, or two weeks. Now that we have learned how to focus on the most relevant price action of a chart, let's continue with more chart patterns that are made with trendlines, support, and resistance.

A **trading range** develops when prices bounce off both a horizontal support and horizontal resistance level. If an uptrend is a consistent increase in price and a downtrend is a consistent decrease in price, then a trading range is a battle between buyers and sellers. It is also sometimes referred to as a narrow sideways channel or **rectangle**, which is an excellent description of what it looks like on a chart.

Consolidation develops when prices begin to trade in a progressively narrower range. As the range narrows, the support and resistance tighten. Typically a consolidation will have an uptrend line and downtrend line forming at the same time, which is commonly referred to as a pennant or **symmetrical triangle**. However, consolidation can also develop with a horizontal support level and downtrend line or a horizontal resistance level and uptrend line. These are called **asymmetrical triangles** (Ch 8.4).

A **downtrend line** is a straight line that is drawn connecting the peaks or swing highs of a market that is falling. The swing highs are also resistance levels. If support is described as a floor, then **resistance** is best described as a ceiling. It's a price area that prices level off at and then move down from. Sellers represent resistance or the ceiling. When sellers feel prices are too high or overvalued, they sell and therefore prevent the market from trading higher. Resistance can be both a diagonal line as in a downtrend or a horizontal line.

While you will hear a common description of uptrends as a series of higher highs and higher lows, it is really just a series of higher lows or support!

Chart 8.4

The same holds true for downtrends, the definition of which is a series of lower highs and lower lows. Again, all that a downtrend really consists of is a series of lower highs or resistance. These are important distinctions because when trading trendlines we wait for breakouts or breakdowns. **Breakouts** occur when prices trade up through a resistance level like a downtrend line or horizontal resistance level. **Breakdowns** occur when prices trade down through an uptrend line or horizontal support level.

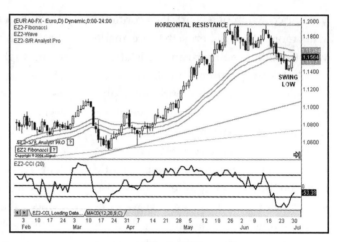

Chart 8.5

What we can see from the support and resistance on this chart is that the market was trading higher and then became overvalued (Ch 8.5). Sellers then stepped in creating resistance, in this case the horizontal level. The market then sold off to a small degree and found some buyers as evident by the most recent swing low.

Just as we can trade breakouts and breakdowns from trendlines, we can use "hits" off support and resistance. Fibonacci levels are also support and resis-

tance (Ch 8.6). A hit can be described as when prices reach an established resistance or support level, and turn in the opposite direction. *Think of a ball bouncing.* A hit off a resistance level would be shown as prices trading upwards to a ceiling only to find sellers at that level and then trade lower from there. If this level is approached and rejected a number of times (at very least once before, preferably twice) we should draw a line at this level, which we will then call resistance.

Many of you are familiar with chart patterns. You may be familiar with channels, triangles, head and shoulders, wedges, and pennants. These are all just different formations of support, resistance, uptrends, and downtrends. The reason I make this distinction is because that's the way I taught myself to find patterns and also because I noticed a particularly interesting phenomenon early on when I begin teaching.

When I would teach a lesson on, for example, triangles, I noticed that suddenly students would notice triangles everywhere. Whatever they were charting, there was a triangle, *whether it was there or not!* It finally dawned on me that with a new way to view the charts, they would inevitably find only what existed in their knowledge base. Of course, what else could they refer to? Their minds were on triangles because I gave them a new concept with which to view the chart. It reminded me of something that I heard a first-year medical student do. Whether it's true or not, I don't know, but it's an interesting study in human behavior. First-year medical students learn about disorders and diseases and the symptoms of each. As they learn of these symptoms, they will tend to view any

Chart 8.6

symptom they notice to be those diseases they study about, no matter how rare or unlikely. You see? That's the framework or the "mental matrix" by which they process information. And as traders, we're the same way. So rather than learning each chart pattern individually, it is best to understand what support, resistance, uptrend, or downtrend lines combine to make each chart pattern first. In that way, there are no limitations to what we will see, and we will not force the patterns onto the chart.

Many times you will come face to face with a chart that has more than one chart pattern forming on it. Take a look at this chart of the euro on a daily chart. We have lines and levels forming a sideways narrow channel or rectangle, a symmetrical triangle (or "pennant"), and two asymmetrical triangles all on the same daily chart (Ch 8.7)!

In these situations, traders can pick and choose which setup suits their risk tolerance and which formation they feel more comfortable trading. I approach these common situations by typically taking the first breakout or breakdown level because we are definitely looking for a momentum trade setup. However, an effective option I will frequently employ would be to use any relevant Fibonacci levels, if available. When there is a breakout/breakdown level that coincides a Fibonacci Level, you have excellent confirmation. *Be on the lookout for anytime you can use this confirmation!*

Another common view of multiple lines and levels occurs when we have more than one

Chart 8.7

set of uptrends and downtrends creating a symmetrical triangle. I will treat these setups the same way as when I have multiple patterns forming (Ch 8.8).

Chart 8.8

Rallies and sell-offs can also be measured and predicted! And much like how we have now learned to draw support and resistance, uptrends, and downtrends, we can also draw retracement levels.

Imagine that you are waiting to enter the market if prices trade above the downtrend or prices trade below the uptrend (Ch 8.8). *Where would you place your profit target? How far is the market most likely to go before it bounces?* Once you learn to draw Fibonacci levels you will see how precisely you will be able answer these questions!

CHAPTER 9

The Difference Between Major and Minor Trendlines

The Difference Between Major and Minor Trendlines

W e've spent some time discussing not just trendlines, but major and minor trendlines. I mark major trendlines with a thicker line width than minor trendlines.

Even though both types of trendlines can confirm a breakout or breakdown, we place more importance on the major trendlines. Here's how I differentiate between the two:

Each trendline is assigned a score based upon four criteria: total length, number of touchpoints, continuity of touchpoints, and proximity to current price. I am not literally taking score; rather I am comparing the available trendlines to one another. I am looking to see how long the trendline is from the first touchpoint to the last. I am counting how many total touchpoints make up the trendline. I am looking for gaps, or major and sudden rallies, and sell-offs. Finally I want to see how close the trendline is to current prices. The trendline that has the highest overall score (based upon the relative weighting of the four criteria) will be drawn thicker and thus be a major uptrend or downtrend line.

If you look at the two uptrends on the CAD A0-FX daily chart (Ch 9.1), you'll see we have one major uptrend and one minor uptrend. If we begin analyzing the lines with the four criteria, we can begin to make the distinction between a major and minor line. *It's a comparative analysis.* In other words, it depends upon the other trendlines on the chart and how they score with the four criteria. The major uptrend line on the chart has three touch points that connect it: January '04, March '04, and April '04. The fact that there are a total of three touchpoints (number of touchpoints criteria), and that the first two were three months apart (total length criteria), help make it a major trendline in comparison to the minor trendline. It is also closer to current price, so it scores better on the proximity comparison. The minor uptrend line has its first touchpoint also in January '04 and a second touchpoint in April '04 for a total of two touchpoints. The time frame between each touchpoint is certainly as long as the major trendline. The reasons that the separate the two are:

1. The major trendline has a total of three touchpoints.
2. It is also closer to current price when compared to the minor trendline.

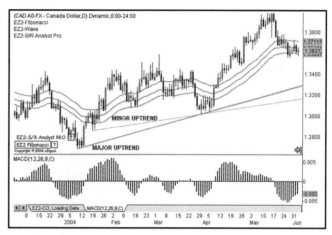

Chart 9.1

CHAPTER 10

Fibonacci Levels

Fibonacci Levels

Most of us initially get into the trading game as a way to improve and take control of our financial lives.

Let's discuss a rule that I live by:

My tools must answer the three questions I ask myself when setting up a trade:

(1) Where to enter the market?
(2) Where to set my profit targets?
(3) Where to set my stop-loss?

Listen to me now; believe me later. From experience I can tell you that the market has taught me this fact, ruthlessly.

Most of us initially get into the trading game as a way to improve and take control of our financial lives. Sooner or later though it becomes all-consuming to see just how good we can be! If you're anything like me, you're either already totally addicted to the market...or you will be. And then we're off to the races to find the best system, tools, indicators, books, videos, software—you name it—that will reveal the secret to trading.

Some of you may have already gone down that slippery slope; others have just begun. *We all do it.* My mom repeatedly told me while growing up me that smart people will learn from their own mistakes but wise people will learn from other people's mistakes. The Holy Grail doesn't exist. At least not the way we think it does.

Here's the "secret" to successful trading: Use time-tested tools consistently with sound trade and risk management. *That's it.* The market is very much a natural phenomenon in that it is a reflection of our fear, greed, and emotion. Since human behavior can be studied and predicted to a fairly accurate degree, so can the behavior of the markets. How many times have you said to someone, "I knew you were going to do that!"? More often than not...that's how the market is too.

One of the best trading tools I use is a mathematical formula discovered by a man named Leonardo da Pisa, *aka* Fibonacci. A scientist and mathematician, Fibonacci was not seeking how to better trade the markets because it did not exist in his lifetime. Born in 1175 AD, he is best known for a series of numbers, later named Fibonacci numbers. The numbers occurred so frequently in nature that the series is commonly referred to as a law of nature. While it is not really a law, it is at very least a very strong tendency.

Fibonacci numbers can be used to explain the number of petals on a flower, the spirals of a nautilus shell, the bumps on a pineapple, the scales of an acorn, the incline of the Egyptian pyramids, even the rate at which cells multiply. Geometry, architecture, and nature all share a tendency to act and react within the mathematical framework of Fibonacci numbers. Since human beings are part of nature, and the financial markets are a reflection of human behavior, we can track the ebb and flow of the markets with Fibonacci numbers.

So what does this have to do with trading Forex? *Glad you asked.* Starting with zero and one, then adding the last number to the sum of the previous two numbers to get the next number forms the Fibonacci number series.

> 0 + 1 (last number) = 1 (sum)
> 1 + 1 = 2
> 1 + 2 = 3
> 3 + 2 = 5

and so on until you get the string
0, 1, 1, 2, 3, 5, 8, 13, 21, 34, 55, 89, 144 ...

For trading purposes we use the values derived by dividing the numbers next to each other in the string by their sum. Those values create the following Fibonacci retracement and extension levels that traders have come to commonly use:

0.250, 0.382, 0.500, 0.618, 0.886, 0.786, 1.000, 1.272, 1.618, 1.886

Fibonacci levels from 0.000 to 1.000 are called **retracements**. The levels above the 1.000 level are called **extensions** as they extend beyond 1.000, or a "full retracement."

Now that we know what retracements and extensions are, let's get to some practical application of these levels. As traders, we must be able to identify and react to retracements levels, which are pullbacks or bounces within the movement of a market. **Pullbacks** and **bounces** occur after a market has made a rally or sell-off. Profit taking most often creates a correction on the chart, and if it occurs within an uptrend, it is called a *pullback*. If it occurs within a downtrend, it is called a *bounce*. The levels at which pullbacks and bounces occur will be the price levels at which we can take profits, place our stop-loss, or even confirm entries. Furthermore, knowing where these levels are before we place a trade allows us to plan ahead and decide risk/reward ratios; this is the vital step of determining whether we will take the trade in the first place.

Note: There is no shortage of charting platforms. Most charting platforms will allow you to draw retracement and extensions and do the calculations for you. They are as easy to draw as finding the two swings you would like to connect using a drag and drop tool to find the Fibonacci levels. I personally use eSignal because it allows me to add the Fibonacci numbers I would like to use, draw multiple levels, and easily delete levels I do not want to use.

Fibonacci retracement and extension levels can show us price levels that we may employ to enter or exit the market; moreover, they can confirm breakouts and breakdowns. Fibonacci retracement and extension levels are really just support and resistance. When a market begins to bounce from a significant decline or pullback from a major rally, the prices will do so most often at Fibonacci numbers. These levels are the retracement of the most recent trend, or last major move. The **last major move** can be measured from the recent swing high to recent swing low. This would be a purely visual way of measuring, much like the peaks and valleys we would use when drawing trendlines, support, and resistance. However, Fibonacci retracement and extension levels are probably not more widely used because of the perception that drawing these levels can be difficult. There is a lot of confusion and misinformation when it comes to how to draw these levels or finding the last major move. The first rule of trading is to be able to see the whole picture. If you use the *look back* settings we use when drawing trendlines to view the most relevant block of time on the chart, the significant swings from which you can begin drawing Fibonacci retracement and extension levels will become obvious. Another key to success when drawing Fibonacci retracement and extension levels is to draw a couple of them and get a feel for how they look. In other words, try a few different swing high and low points. There are always multiple Fibonacci retracement and extension

levels on a chart. The
common misconception
is that there is a right
one. All we are looking
for is the most relevant
and recent. The most rel-
evant Fibonacci retrace-
ment and extension level
will have secondary con-
firmation. It will coordi-
nate with breakout and
breakdown levels, it will
line up with other sup-
port and resistance lev-

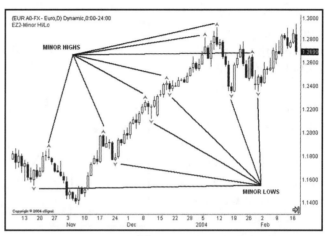

Chart 10.1

els, "psychological," or round numbers,
etc. Until you are able to train your eyes
to see these accurately and easily, let's
explore another way of finding swings
with a simple chart pattern: minor highs
and minor lows.

Finding Minor Highs and Minor Lows

Minor highs and minor lows are not complex patterns. (These are not to be confused with swings or pivots as minor
highs and minor lows have a specific
chart pattern that must form.) With a little practice, minor highs and minor lows
will seem to pop out of your charts.
Because an uptrend is a series of higher
lows and a downtrend is a series of lower
highs, I find that minor highs and minor
lows identify the individual highs and

lows within the overall trend (Ch 10.1).
Consider this: An uptrend is simply support, while a downtrend is resistance.

The concept of minor highs and
minor lows is certainly nothing new. I
first began testing these patterns when
I read about them back in late 1989. When
looking for a minor high, you are looking for a current high that has a lower
high before and after it. Minor lows occur
when a current low has a higher low
before and after it. These patterns show
us where prices are likely to change direction as in a swing or pivot. Often you
will see there are minor highs and minor
lows in close proximity to one another
on the chart. In situations like these,
simply use the highest minor high or the
lowest minor low.

Minor high and minor low patterns consist of three candles, end-of-day or intraday. Ignore inside ranges. (Inside ranges, also known as "inside days," are those candles whose trading range is within the previous day's range.) Let's take a look at the circled section of this daily chart of the euro (Ch 10.2A).

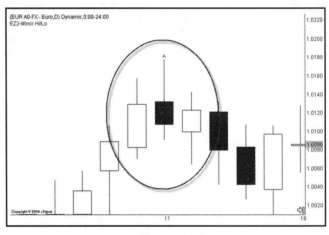

Chart 10.2A

As you can see, we were alerted to this minor high because prices first established a new high, marked by the carrot symbol above that candle's high. Once we establish a new high, we go back to the preceding candle to see whether it had a lower high and lower low. If it did, that is day 1 of your pattern, and the new high is day 2. Next we need to see a day 3 candle that has a lower high and lower low compared to the range of day 2. If we do, we have a confirmed minor high (Ch. 10.2B).

With these minor highs and minor lows we can begin to draw Fibonacci retracement and extension levels because we have all the high and low pivots marked on the chart with a specific criteria. These highs and lows lay out the last major moves.

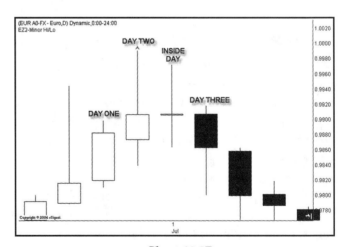

Chart 10.2B

Since we are looking for the "last major move," which is the most recent rally or decline, we will focus on the move from the highest, most recent minor high to the lowest, most recent minor low.

The pattern will take on a slightly different look when there is an inside day, but the concept is still the same. Our goal is the find the reversals of trend that make up a "last major move" which is simply an un-retraced rally or sell-off (Ch 10.2B). Once you have drawn your Fibonacci levels based upon the last major move, you will see that you now have support and resistance levels that will help you determine where the market is most likely to move to next. Remember that if you are looking for upside resistance, you are looking for the last major sell-off and if you are looking for downside support, you are looking for the last major rally (Ch 10.3). Personally, I think of Fibonacci levels as the mathematical explanation of the saying that for every action there is an opposite reaction.

Chart 10.3

There are other ways of locating swings or pivots. And while the definitions may differ from trader to trader, you can use a point-based measurement or even a percentage-based measurement. One simple way would be to find new highs that are followed by two subsequent lower closes or new lows that are followed by two subsequent higher closes. The high or low createdwould qualify as a pivot or swing. Whatever way you decide to begin finding swing highs and swing lows from which to draw your Fibonacci levels, just remember that the best way to learn is to practice, practice, practice!

CHAPTER 11
Visual Tools

Visual Tools

I'm going to now share with you how I use those trio of lines traveling across my charts. From my experience, teaching students from different countries, backgrounds, and education levels, I have found that most of us are visual traders.

What we *see* resonates with us and shapes our opinion of the market. It makes perfect sense. We believe what we see. Charts are visual tools, and much of what we do as we learn to become better traders is train our eyes to notice the small clues the market gives us.

Some of my favorite tools have come from working closely with my students. I love teaching and for a very self-serving reason: It makes me stick to my own rules. I have to walk the talk. I think my students can sniff-out a trader from a wanna-be trader a mile away. I teach using real time charts. If students can see how the setup develops in real time, make the decisions that have to be made in real time, and feel the ebb and flow of the market, they then can begin to understand what it takes to become a trader.

I encourage my students to think outside the box and come to me with ideas they would like to experiment with. Once such an idea came from a student, Dave, who is now a very good friend. I respected Dave's dedication as a student immensely. And now I respect him for being a dedicated trader. I like Dave's take on the world and the markets. So when he came to me about four years ago with a moving average he was trading with, I listened. He was playing with some Fibonacci number-based moving averages, specifically, the 34 EMA. (EMA stands for exponential moving average.) Moving averages (MA) are very popular technical analysis tools that not only smoothe out the major trend in the market but also show support and resistance. Simple MAs calculate and plot the average of a set number of days or periods. For example, a 20-day MA will take the last 20 closing prices and divide them by 20 to plot the average. Moving averages can be calculated for any intraday time frames (e.g. 5, 10, 20 minutes) and also on either the open, high, low, or close. Exponential MAs work much the same way except that they place more emphasis on more recent prices to plot the average.

Chart 11.1

Dave and I experimented with the 34 EMA, and I plotted it on the high, low, and close, as I often will if I am looking at a new MA setting for the first time. The first thing I noticed was that when prices cross the three lines of the high, low, and close, it tended to keep going, and pullbacks or bounces in a trend seemed to come right to one of the three lines. It got my interest, and after keeping the 34 EMA on the high, low, and close on my charts for about six months, they earned a permanent place in my analysis. I did test the entire Fibonacci series all the way up to 144, and 34 tested the best. Thus, the "Dave Wave" was born...we call it the Wave for short (Ch 11.1).

Now it's not a magic bullet—nothing is. Here's how to best use the Wave. First, since there are multiple time frames I could be watching and analyzing, I have to be able to decide which has the best trending characteristics. I will go through the 30-, 60-, 180-, and 240-minute daily charts with the Wave on each chart. This visual tool allows me to quickly see if the market has been trading smoothly above or below the Wave, if the pullbacks or bounces retrace into the Wave, or if the Wave is moving sideways and there is no prevailing trend (Ch 11.2).

You'll notice that some time frames don't adhere to the Wave as well as others in certain market environments. This will vary as market environments change from trending to choppy and back again.

At least once a day I look at each chart with the Wave.

Another helpful trick when using the Wave is what I call "Chris Clock Angles." I was over at my neighbor's house. We were talking about the markets, and I was showing him some of the tools that I had been using, namely, the Wave. I explained to him that I like

Chart 11.2

to see the Wave traveling in "nice rolling hills" where it isn't sloping or climbing too steeply. My neighbor was still a bit fuzzy about my explanation, so I told him he should just a get a feel for the slope of the trend like a nice 45-degree angle for an uptrend, as too steep or shallow a trend is not what we want to see. His son, Chris, was sitting at the table with us, seemingly uninterested in our conversation until he chimed in, "Raghee, isn't that one o'clock?" I looked at Chris—all of 9 or 10 years old at the time—and said "huh?"

"You know, like, one o'clock." He pointed at my laptop screen and showed me what he meant and then added, "and that's five o'clock." It sunk in. The Wave was traveling between noon and two in an uptrend and between four and six o'clock in a downtrend. When the market was stuck in a range it traveled at three o'clock. And I then realized that sometimes it takes a kid to point out the obvious.

Chris Clock Angles allow me to take a visual measurement of whether the market is in a chop or trending. If the market is in a chop I will look for setups like triangle breakouts and rectangles to set up a momentum trade. If the market is trending at Chris Clock Angles, then I will typically look for bounces or pullbacks to set up a swing trade.

The Wave is by far my most important visual tool regarding trading style. As we discuss swing versus momentum trading, you will see that the clock angle of the Wave will have a huge impact on which style we will trade and, more important, whether we will take the trade at all.

CHAPTER 12

Measuring Trends with CCI on Short- and Long-Term Charts

Measuring Trends with CCI on Short- and Long-Term Charts

Even though I prefer not to use indicators alone when deciding upon entries and exits, they can be helpful to *confirm* trends and reversals. Since we have already discussed the Wave as a visual tool, let's talk about another helpful indicator, the Commodity Channel Index.

It's funny to me now, but when I first started trading commodity futures in college, I didn't know much about the futures market at all. My experience until then was solely based on stocks and mutual funds. I understood price action, drew trendlines, support, resistance, Fibonacci levels, etc., but thought that I needed something more for the futures market. One morning, I was looking through the list of indicators on my charting platform and came across the Commodity Channel Index. It seemed so obvious to me at the time that if I was to be a *commodity* futures trader, I needed to use the *Commodity Channel Index* (CCI). So, using a basic setting of 20, I began measuring the momentum and shifts in trend with the CCI.

Donald Lambert developed the Commodity Channel Index (CCI). The CCI measures the price in relation to a moving average. It is an oscillating indicator, thus it signals when the market is overbought/oversold or when a trend is changing. If the CCI is set to 20, which is a typical or "default" setting, price is then measured in relation to a 20-period moving average.

This chart of the EUR A0-FX is on a five-minute timeframe with the Wave plotted on it. *Remember, the Wave is the 34 EMA on the high, low, and close* (Ch 12.1). I have found that you need volatility to register trendlines and trendline breaks on the CCI itself. From my experience, I would have to say that shorter, intraday time frames are more suited to this, but any chart with wider ranges and volatility will do as shown by this daily chart of the JPY A0-FX.

The upper and lower bands on this CCI are set to +100/–100. Now some people like to trade off shorter time frames like the five-minute chart I used as an example earlier. I don't. I'd much rather stick with the "slower" times frames of the 30, 60, 180, 240, and daily when I trade Forex. Since we are trading a 24-hour market there is less of a need to use shorter time frames. Traders involved in the futures or stock markets will often use shorter time frames because they are looking for setups in a market that closes each day and may only trade a few hours like the Cocoa market or 7½ hours like the equities market.

Chart 12.1

And here's something to consider: How *you* like to trade and *your* personality. The truth is there is not just one correct way to trade or one correct time frame! I highly recommend that anyone who wants to be a trader read the *Market Wizards* books by Jack Schwager. Each and every trader in that book is the "real deal." These people walk the talk. What's also interesting to note is that they all don't trade in a similar way...at all! They all have very unique styles, tools, and beliefs. Some are chartists and techni-

cians, some rely on computer models, others are pit traders, and a few use fundamentals. Regardless, they all take money out of the markets on a regular basis.

You need to find what styles, tools, and beliefs you want to adopt and model those traders who have found success with those very same things. Over the years it has become obvious to me that my style is much more breakout/ breakdown oriented. It's just the way I am wired. I like to "stalk" my trades and when the time is right, pounce. Using trendlines, support, resistance, Fibonacci, the Wave, allows me to develop my entire trading plan from entry to stop-loss to profit targets before I enter the trade. But its breakout/ breakdown trading that gives me the feeling of getting in at the beginning of the move as opposed to trading when the trend has already been established. That is not to say I do not like swing or position trading. I am equally comfortable entering an established trend after a pullback or using a consolidation within the context of the trend. I just naturally gravitate to the style that I enjoy and don't think that won't affect the way you look at the charts. Make sure you know your tendencies.

Another aspect to finding your style—as it pertains to your personality—is the time frame you monitor. I personally find that I am not wired to be a scalper. I like an intermediate to long-term time frame. I like momentum and rather not sit through or wait for swings to enter a trade. We'll talk about scalping, momentum, swing, and position trading later in this book. My point is that you should dedicate some time early on to finding the aspects of one particular style that suit three factors: (1) the time you can dedicate to trading, (2) your temperament, (3) your account size or risk capital.

I have found more than anything that the time you have available to dedicate to trading will

have the biggest impact on the style you will succeed with.

Back to the CCI: Contrary to my preferences, it can certainly be a stand-alone to trigger trades on CCI trendline breaks as shown in Charts 12.1 and 12.2. For those of you who feel this might be something you'd like to try, there are a few nuances to watch. Like many other oscillating indicators, there are basically two ways of using the CCI: looking for divergences or as an overbought/oversold indicator. For our purposes, we will use the CCI in its overbought/oversold capacity. Focus on more volatile markets for good trendlines.

There is another chart set up that you may want to consider. It uses the Wave as the entry trigger and the CCI as the confirmation. When looking at less

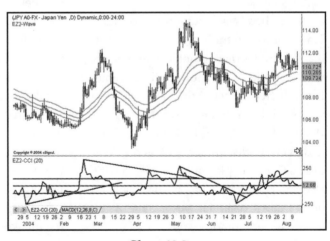

Chart 12.2

volatile or trending markets, you will often see that drawing trendlines on the CCI and then playing the trendline break is not as ideal for the indicator because if volatility isn't there to register good trendlines, it goes against the nature of an oscillating indicator. If you remember Chris Clock Angles you already know how to identify a "good" trendline. Chris Clock Angles apply to trendlines you can draw on the chart or on the CCI. A good uptrend will be between noon and two o'clock and a good downtrend will be between four and six o'clock.

In the Wave/CCI combo set up we would be waiting for prices to make a "clean breakthrough," a Wave that is traveling at Chris Clock Angles. A clean break is when prices trade up through the Wave for the first time. In other words, if prices are already trading below the Wave, then a clean break would be when prices first trade up through it. We call this a "Chris Cross."

The CCI buy confirmation of a clean break up through the Wave would be at least a +100 reading. The sell confir-

mation would then be a clean breakdown through the Wave with a CCI reading of –100.

The two circled areas show the clean breaks or a Chris Cross on this British pound daily chart (Ch 12.3). The arrows on this chart point out where prices retraced back into the Wave and, held as resistance as in the first case and support, with the second. So let's add the CCI confirmation to see how these set ups come together.

Chart 12.3 shows the same clean break circles as the first example chart, but now we look to the CCI for confirmation of the clean break (Ch 12.4). The upper bands represent +100 while the lower band is –100. Those levels are our "line in the sand." If the CCI reading is between

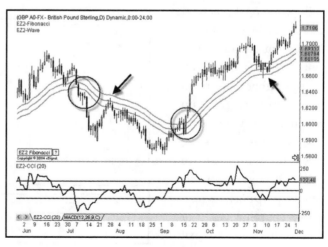

Chart 12.3

+100 and −100 then we have a neutral reading, which we do not act on. For a short trade we need a clean break with a CCI reading of at least −100. For a long trade we need a clean break with a CCI reading of least +100. These are entry rules only. Trade management is done with mainly Fibonacci levels, so let's take a quick look at the chart with all the tools active (Ch 12.5).

Chart 12.4

Now we can see the uptrend line, and more important, we can see support and resistance levels from the Fibonacci levels. This is especially important as we can see the 1.272 Level will be the next potential resistance level, and the 1.000 should hold as support if prices intend on going higher. The main idea here is to give you an another way of entering a trade; however, keep in mind that we will still use Fibonacci levels, support, resistance, "psychological" or round numbers, to exit at our profit targets.

And we'll definitely cover more in depth the above mentioned in Chap. 18, Three Classic Tools to a Three-Step Setup and Chap. 20, Rewriting Trade Management.

Chart 12.5

CHAPTER 13

Trading Versus Investing

Trading Versus Investing

While it may seem like semantics, it's a matter of goals and methods. Trading and investing are two very distinct ways of engaging the markets.

Most simply put, trading is what's most commonly considered buying low and selling high (and for a short trade selling high and buying back low). Trading is all about looking to profit form a market's ebb and flow, from its rallies and declines.

On the other side of the coin is investing. One of the most commonly used and best examples of investing are mutual funds. Most people with a 401K or IRA have mutual funds. With these you own shares of the fund and typically invest a set dollar amount each month or with each paycheck. There is no timing or consideration of price involved in dollar-cost average-based purchases. Accumulating these shares, increasing one's "ownership" of the fund or a specific stock, is investing. Your goal is to accumulate more and more shares. Of course there is the expectation that the value of the shares will increase; however, the main goal of investing is to accumulate shares or ownership, commonly by dollar-cost averaging, regardless of price.

Most market participants believe they are investors. The connotation of investing is one of value-based purchases, prudence, and safety. On the other hand, most people think of trading as a high-risk activity, more akin to gambling than carefully calculated market timing.

Contrary to popular opinion, a trade can be a two-minute, two-hour or two-year event. The goal of trading is to time an entry and exit in such a way that you can profit from the subsequent price movement. The length of time in the market doesn't differentiate a trade from an investment. It's the goal that separates the two. "Dollar-cost averaging" is something an investor does, and with good reason, as it is the means to their end, which is to accumulate more shares or contracts. Dollar-cost averaging is investing money at a set time (usually monthly) regardless of price and market condition. When you think about investing, think about ownership. A trader would not (and should not!) even consider this as it is contrary to the timing and price based entries that govern trading.

Another point that separates traders from investors is the stop-loss and heat. What is *heat*? Heat is the amount of points or money a trader will allow a position to go against him or her. Heat is not a consideration to an investor, as dollar-cost averaging does not take into account price or market condition. Where a trader may exit the trade based on price, an investor will be accumulating more shares at a reduced price thereby reducing their cost basis. Cost basis is the average cost of all shares or contracts owned. If an investor bought 10 shares at $20 and 10 more shares at $30, then the cost basis of all 20 shares would be $25.

Stop-losses are what keeps a trader in business: admitting that you were wrong and moving on. There is a set of reasons for traders entering the market, and when those reasons are no longer valid, they should exit the trade. A stop-loss must be adhered to at all times. A stop-loss simply represents the price level at which the trade is no longer valid, where the reasons to be in the

trade have been broken. Traders are not interested in ownership. And investors are not concerned with heat or interested in stop-losses to manage the investment.

Why are these important distinctions? One of the most dangerous scenarios in a trade is letting the rules and goals of investing to creep in. Many of us have been there. We hang onto what was to be a short-term trade too long, waiting for it to turn around, and before we know it that short-term trade becomes an investment. We must go into each position knowing what our goals are because each of the two goals comes with their own set of rules and goals.

If your goal is to buy low and sell high, you are a trader and price and timing are your concerns. Trading is an income producing activity. An activity, that if done well, will allow you to invest in various ways. If your end goal is growth of shares or ownership, you're an investor and dollar-cost averaging is typically the method.

I am not here to pass judgment on trading or investing. What I do want you to realize is that each is a powerful way to financial success, in their different ways. Even though I have dedicated this book to the practice of trading, I recommend doing both and diversifying your portfolio and approach to the markets.

CHAPTER 14

The Funnel Mindset

The Funnel Mindset

We are bombarded with information daily. It is our job to sift through what is relevant and what is not in order for us to function day in and day out. Trading is nothing different.

When you factor in newsletters, television, radio, and the Internet, there is no shortage of opinion and commentary that we are exposed to, whether we like it or not. Some of it is tempting and intriguing, but it's our job as traders to stay true to what we know works for us, and to stay true to our plan. Right now, where you sit in your home, office, wherever, you have dozens of noises and sensations around you: *Maybe you have the radio or television on; a fan or air conditioner might be on blowing cool air; the sun is shining or you are sitting near a lamp; maybe dinner is cooking and you smell that aroma; a dog could be barking; a car could be honking.* And we are deleting most, if not all, of that out. We have to! Our mind, consciously and unconsciously, focuses on what we need to. Each day we have to do that same thing when we engage the markets. However, you and I must consciously decide upon what we will allow our mind to focus on.

The Funnel Mindset is what we adopt to consciously to take in all the information we're exposed to and purposely filter it down to the points that will allow us to build our trade. Imagine pouring in all the information in your mind about the market and a particular trade into a funnel; maybe it's one that you're considering now. The overall trend, the patterns, Fibonacci, indicators, and reports, these are all items that will effect our final decision. As all this information is traveling down our mental "funnel" as we narrow the information down and prioritize what will serve our immediate needs to enter or exit a trade. There are three items that we need to decide upon before entering any trade:

1. The entry
2. Potential profit targets
3. Potential stop-loss levels

It's natural to be curious about factors that may seem relevant to our trade, but it's imperative that we filter out everything that doesn't directly lead us to an entry or exit price. *So how do we filter the unnecessary information out?* We ask questions. But what questions do we ask?

The "Ands" and the "Ors"

Entering a trade is a process of asking and answering questions: *Is the trend up or down? Is the market choppy? Are prices trading above or below the Wave? Am I waiting for a pullback or bounce, or am I waiting for a breakout or breakdown? Am I setting up a momentum trade or a swing trade? Where are my swing highs and swing lows? Did my Fibonacci retracement and extension level give me secondary confirmation? Have my trendlines, support, and resistance levels formed a chart pattern? Are there any reports to be released today?* These are just some of the questions I ask myself when I am trading. If you have ever driven a manual transmission car you remember when shifting gears was a very conscious set of step-by-step actions: *Take my foot off the gas, push in the clutch, hold it while I shift, take my foot off the clutch without stalling, get back on the gas.* Soon you did it all without consciously thinking about each step. The "ands" and the "ors" are the same way.

Entering the market is always done with a set of "ands." In other words, more than just one thing has to happen for us to enter a trade, preferably two or three things. For example, an upside trendline break for a momentum set up may require that the trendline breaks *and* is not trading too close to a Fibonacci level that may act as resistance *and* has either a sideways or noon to two o'clock Wave, *and* I am not trading in front of a economic report, *and* my risk/reward ratio is at least 1:1 or better. If any one of these criteria weren't where we needed it to be, we would not take the trade. Think of an airplane taking off and the checklist a pilot goes through. If one item on the checklist isn't okay, the plane won't take off.

Exiting a trade is done with just an "or." And remember exits can be both stop-loss exits and profit targets. For example, if you took the upside breakout we were just discussing and prices are now trading at the first profit target, that alone is enough to exit. In this case you will exit out of one or more of your lots. Let's say that the breakout failed and prices are now trading at your stop-loss...again. That too is reason enough to exit! So your mindset for exits will be whether my profit target was hit *or* my stop-loss was hit *or* an economic report is going to be released so I don't want to be in the market *or* I am nearing a "psychological" or round number...so I want to exit one or more of my lots. A **lot** is like a share of stock or a contract in the commodity futures market; it is simply one unit.

Sadly enough some traders in an overeager attempt to make money will overtrade. You will notice that losing traders will use "ors" to enter markets and "ands" to exit them! Just ask them what needs to happens for them to enter or exit a trade, and you will begin to understand the questions they ask themselves to qualify their actions. If you find yourself doing this, dump a bucket of cold water over your head and snap out of it! (Just don't do it near your computer.)

CHAPTER 15

The Difference Between Scalping, Momentum, Swing, and Position Trading

The Difference Between Scalping, Momentum, Swing, and Position Trading

Let's begin this discussion with the understanding that the definition of scalping, momentum, swing, and position trading will vary from trader to trader.

We need a baseline so I will describe each of these trading types as it pertains to how you may want to incorporate each into your approach to the markets and also which you find you may begin to adopt more actively into your trading day. There is one idea—I should say one myth—that needs to be dispelled. Trading types have nothing to do with how long you are in a trade. The idea that a trade is defined by the time spent in the market is ridiculous. Trade types are defined by how you enter a trade, not by its duration. There are only two reasons to exit a trade: because your stop-loss was reached or because your profit target was reached. The time it takes to do either is irrelevant. With that said, we'll cover scalping first.

Scalping, in my opinion, is an "advanced" type of trading, not because of the style itself, but because the speed at which you must be able to recognize the trade set up and execute the order.

Scalping is often the best choice for floor or pit traders since they have a unique vantage point and the quickest execution response to order flow. Scalping is typically done using very short-term intervals, like one-minute or tick charts. This is because scalpers want to be out before the slightest pullback. Scalp trades are done in the direction of the current trend and allow a trader to take small "bites" of the overall move. Scalpers may enter and exit a number of times along the same trend taking small pieces as the trend persists. Scalpers may not be the first ones in the trend, but they are always the first ones out. Quick thinking and quick reflexes prevail, and an error in judgment can often wipe out an entire day's profit.

If I sound a little down on scalping, that's my experience and personality coming through. It's my least favorite style. But let me add that quite a few of my close trading friends and partners are world-class scalpers and there are many people who enjoy the action and are comfortable with this style of trading. I just happen to not be one of them. If you are a new trader, please humor me and learn to momentum, swing, or position trade first then go seek the tutelage of an experienced and successful scalper when you are ready.

The next style we'll discuss is momentum trading. As I have mentioned before, this is my favorite style but not because I consciously chose it. I think you will discover that many times your style will choose you! Momentum traders wait for breakouts and breakdowns as a clear signal to a shift in momentum, coming out of a trading range or consolidation. Traders that prefer to trade chart patterns like triangles, pennants, and narrow sideways channels are typically momentum traders. Momentum traders stay in the trade for the duration of the trend's momentum and consequently will not sit through significant pullbacks. Which brings us to swing trading.

Swings can be defined as the pullbacks in uptrends and the bounces in downtrends. Swing trading is predicated upon the belief that once a trend is established it will continue until the trend shifts in the other direction and reverses. Swing traders will buy pullbacks in an established uptrend and short bounces in an established downtrend; chart analysis will show us specifically when to do so.

Swing trading is the best way to enter established trends since you will not buy into the highs or short into the lows. In fact, if you missed an initial entry in your momentum trade, it is often best to put on your "swing trading hat" and wait for a pullback or bounce if the trend continues.

When you have exited out of your entire position, that is what's called being "flat." A sell-stop is your stop-loss in an uptrend and would exit you from a long position; and a buy-stop is your stop-loss in a downtrend and would exit you from a short position. One idea I encourage all traders to adopt is to look at the market from both directions. When you are looking at a buy, take just a moment to see what someone who is thinking of selling might be seeing. Always, take a moment to step in the shoes of a trader who may be on the other side of your trade. Many people who come from an investing background will typically only look at the markets from the long side or as buyers. Doing this severely limits the opportunities that are available to you in any market. Professional traders sell short as frequently and as comfortably as the buy long. For those of you who may not be completely familiar with shorting, it is simply taking a trade that allows you to profit as a market falls. When we go long, we buy contracts in expectation of rising prices. We will eventually sell them and realize our profit. Conversely, when we short a market, we sell contacts in expectation of falling prices. We will eventually buy back these contracts and realize our profit if the market is lower than when we initially sold it. What I'd like you to come away with here is that each style has it's own rules. The entry rules are what distinguish one trading style from another.

Let's take a look at an example of a swing trade, and a momentum trade. Ch 15.1 shows the pullbacks within the uptrend. In this case we are looking a pullbacks to the Wave. You may of course use Fibonacci levels as well; personally I prefer the Wave. Just keep in mind that we are looking for "measured pullbacks or bounces." A measure pullback is simply a price level that we have determined before entering the trade will offer support or resistance within the context of the current

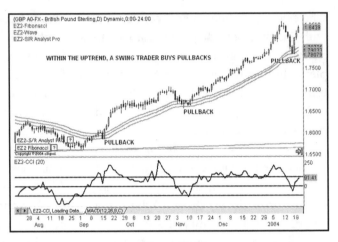

Chart 15.1

trend. Measure pullbacks can also include psychological or "round numbers." Ch 15.2 shows the support of the uptrend line and the resistance of the downtrend line forming a triangle.

Chart 15.2

CHAPTER 16

Two Cornerstone Steps of Trade Setups

Two Cornerstone Steps of Trade Setups

T*he cornerstone of my trading can be summarized in two easy steps:*
(1) Find the trend: short and long term.
(2) Find potential reversals within the trend.

Let's explore this further because this is the mindset behind each of my trades. Now this may sound remedial—if not outright obvious—but a trade is made up of three points:

1. An entry
2. Potential profit targets
3. Potential stop-loss levels

I use three tools to support these decisions: Fibonacci levels, trendlines (including support and resistance), and my trend indicator, *aka* the Wave. Here's an example of a typical chart. On this daily chart of symbol EUR A0-FX, there are three tools active on this chart (Ch 16.1).

First, let's look at the Wave plotted by the triple lines. Next we can look at the two trendlines on this chart, and finally the Fibonacci levels on the right side.

So how do these tools help me reach a decision on my three points?

Since we've already talked about how a trade begins with the process of asking and answering questions, the first question I ask myself is whether I am on the "weak" or "strong" side of the trend. Looking to see whether the market is trading above or below the Wave easily accomplishes this. On this chart (Ch 16.1) you can see that we are on the weak side of the trend. Weak means that a short would be with the trend, while a long would be against the trend. We will cover this in great detail when we discuss Prep Work, Chap. 17.

The second question involves finding potential reversals within the trend. In order to pinpoint profit targets and stop-loss levels I must decide upon where I think the trend is most likely to reverse. A reversal in the direction of my trade will set up my profit targets while reversals in the opposite direction of my trade are the areas I will look to place stop-loss orders above or below. For example, if I were in a long trade, my stop-loss would be placed just below a support level, while my profit targets will be placed approximately five pips below the resistance levels. I use Fibonacci levels to accomplish this. These levels allow me to find support and resistance levels within the context of the trend, or the "last major move."

The next chart of the 60-minute euro shows how this works. (Ch 16.2) The last major move in this case was from 1.2389 to 1.2173. The price level of 1.2173 represents a 1.000 or full retracement, while the 1.2389 level represents the end of the "last major move," which in this case was a rally. The price action that comes after the 0.000 level is now considered a retracement.

Therefore, the Fibonacci levels on the right side of Chart 16.2 show where this market is most likely to trade to and then potentially find support and resistance. *(When working with support and resistance, like Fibonacci levels, what was once support becomes resistance when prices trade below it and what was once resistance becomes support when prices trade above it.)* With the gradual drop from the high (the 0.000 level), we can see that the market found short-term sup-

Chart 16.1

port at the 0.250 then the 0.382 Fibonacci levels and then sliced through the 0.382. The 0.500 level finally brought some support. In a hypothetical trade, each level could have been a potential entry or profit target for a short. (Remember, I am only

Chart 16.2

considering trade management here. These are not entry rules.)

Since we know the rules that govern past support and resistance level, these levels have not outlived their usefulness yet! Now each one of these potential support levels are all potential *resistance*. But Fibonacci Levels are not the only support and resistance we should watch for. Currently we see that the downtrend line is holding prices from trading higher (Ch 16.3).

Think of horizontal support and resistance levels like a multistory building. Each floor is a support and each ceiling is resistance. However, what may be one person's ceiling is the floor for someone above. That's how support and resistance works, so it is important to watch them going up and down. I can also use these levels as stop-losses. For example, a short entry could have one of the profit targets at the 0.250 Fibonacci level. *(I like to place my orders at least five pips above in a short.)* since prices bounced there, so now the 1.000 Fibonacci level could be a ceiling or resistance, and also a stop-loss if I had more of the position left and wanted to protect my profits.

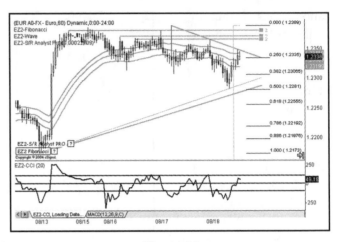

Chart 16.3

Let's discuss some distinctions about entries. **Entries depend upon whether we are momentum trading or swing trading.** For momentum trades we will use trendline, support, or resistance breakouts or breakdowns. For swing trades we will rely on pullbacks or bounces, otherwise known as retracements. These retracements will most often be to Fibonacci levels or the Wave and occasionally to trendlines, support, or resistance lines. Regardless of your entry type, I have found that mos trades are made or broken by the exits. Entries are the easy part. Now this does not mean that we are allowed to enter late or with sloppy execution and chase trades. It's just that I have seen, time after time, that well-timed exits are what oftentimes makes the difference between pocketing a profit and breaking even. Exits come in two types: profit targets and stop-losses.

Exits must be supported by price action. If a trader enters a market based on the chart, then any exit—profit or loss—should also be based on the chart. This is why I am always searching the charts following my two steps: *(1) Find the trend: short and long term. (2) Find potential reversals within the trend.*

With this philosophy in mind, let's take a look at a current view with all the analysis so that you can make some decisions of your own. Check out the chart of the EUR A0-FX on the 60-minute time frame with the Fibonacci levels, trendlines, and the Wave (Ch 16.4).

As you look at this chart I want you to think about a few things:

The Wave is neutral (moving at three o'clock). See how it's more sideways and that prices are trading within it rather than above or below? Are we setting up a potential momentum or swing

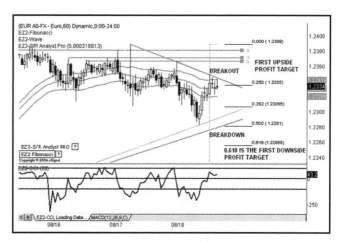

Chart 16.4

trade? If prices break out, what level is your stop-loss at and where will your first profit target be? What if prices break down?

Here's how I would analyze it (Ch 16.5).

Chart 16.5

CHAPTER 17

"Prep Work"

"Prep Work"

Before beginning the "three classic steps" of building a trade, there is one step that we all must do, and that's make sure we're looking at the best time frame.

Even though this is relatively easy "prep work," it makes a huge difference in the quality of the trades. Consider this the foundation of all trades.

Finding the overall trend on each time frame, even if making a mental note, is key. I like to write this info on an index card. In fact, I write down all relevant numbers for any trade set up on a 3 x 5 index card. This means that I write the five time frames that I scan on each index card. These are the 30, 60, 180, 240, and daily. (*There are other time frames that you can look at as well. These are typically very short time frames like the 5-, 10-, or 15-minute charts. I prefer not to trade on time frames that short, but the tools work on all time frames.*) Next to each time frame I will draw a small arrow to show the prevailing trend, whether that be an uptrend, downtrend, or a sideways market which would show no trend: # $ 1.

This first step can be accomplished quickly and accurately with the Wave.

Remember the Wave is a 34 EMA on a high, close, and low. With the Wave plotted on each of the time frame, we want to take a quick visual account of the quality of the trend. When I say "quality" I mean: At what "clock angle" is the trend climbing or falling? Has the market made a retracement? No trend goes straight up or down, they all retrace at some point. Retracements are those pullbacks in an uptrend or bounces in a downtrend. Look for trends trend that climb with the Wave and retrace back into the lines of the Wave. The retracement may not be perfect, but as you do this over and over again on different pairs and time frames you will be able to tell good Wave retracements from bad ones. Be conscious of the fact that you are now training your eyes to notice certain things. Notice the way a trend climbs after an initial breakout or how it looks as it weakens. When the trend does retrace, does it pull back before the Wave or does it trade through the Wave like it wasn't even there?

Let's look at some examples. This first example is of the euro on a 60-minute interval (Ch 17.1). We use the *look back* numbers to get a proper read on the current trading environment. (If you need to refer to the appropriate look back for each time frame,

Chart 17.1

revisit How to Draw Trendlines.) The five trading days in this example show where prices have retraced into the Wave in the downtrend. The last test on June 14 shows a clean crossing of price through the Wave and thus the downtrend was broken as measured by the Wave. Notice that the retracement we see during these five days went right into and not beyond the top line of the Wave. These retracements are exactly what we want to short in an established downtrend when we are swing trading.

The next example is the British Pound on the daily chart (Ch 17.2). In this case we have gone back to the first week of July '03. When looking at the Wave on a daily chart, I will typically go to the most recent trend change or "Chris

Cross" through the Wave. This allows me to see any retracements as well as how and where the trend began which will allow me to make a decision as to whether I will be setting up a momentum or swing trade.

In this case there was a "Chris Cross" in mid-September '03. The uptrend that followed retraced into the Wave three times during the uptrend. This example shows that the uptrend followed the Wave and that the retracements did not break the bottom line of the Wave. These retracements are exactly what we want to buy in an established uptrend when we are swing trading.

Now let's a take a look at a market that is not following the Wave, thus making it a time frame that currently would not qualify as a trending market. Of course, this does not mean we will not consider a set on this chart, it simply narrows down the choice to momentum trading. In this case we can revisit this chart and mark our trendlines, support, and resistance line to take note of any triangles, pennants, or rectangles that might be forming.

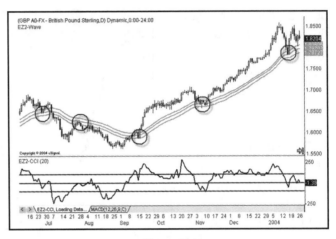

Chart 17.2

The arrows on the next chart example the British pound on a daily chart show many Wave breaks (Chart 17.3). This tells us two things: first, the trend is not a smooth one, and second, there is too much chop to safely enter a swing trade. This brings up a powerful point.

When the Wave is haphazardly broken into the upside and downside without a subsequent trend, the market is most likely trading a range or "chop," which means we will watch the chart for a possible momentum trade.

This next chart of the euro on a daily time frame shows what happens when the Wave is moving sideways (Ch 7.4). We can see that prices are stuck in a range and certainly not ideal for swing

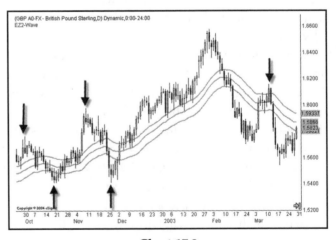

Chart 17.3

trading. Remember Chris Clock Angles? The chart shows an angle of three o'clock. If the Wave is not traveling at between noon and two o'clock for an uptrend, or between four o'clock and six o'clock for a downtrend, we should stay away from swing trading. And here's another important point: Just because the Wave is not ideal for one

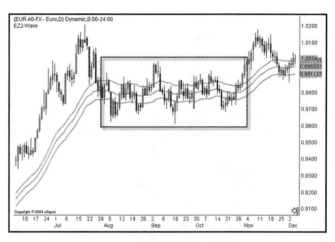

Chart 17.4

type of trade doesn't mean that we should give up on that market altogether, we will simply move on to the next of our five time frames. We are can scan through the 30- 60-, 180-, 240- minute, and daily charts.

Markets follow a four- phase cycle (Ch 17.5). As traders we look to differ- entiate the up and down- trends, which are ideal for swing trading, from the sideways trend. First, the Wave and, second, drawing trendlines, sup- port, and resistance help us to this very effectively. When a market begins to lose momentum at the

end of an uptrend (also called *markup*) it will many times transition into a choppy phase we call *distribution*. The distribu- tion is typically volatile. At the end of a downtrend (also called *markdown*) the

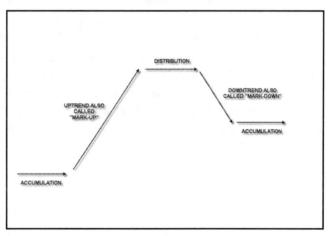

Chart 17.5

market will also tend to enter a choppy phase called *accumulation*, which is markedly less volatile than distribution. Both these phases are more suited to momentum trading.

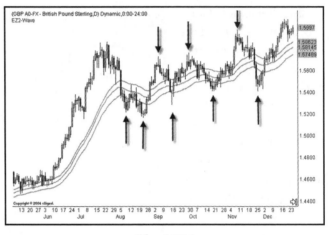

Chart 17.6

Last, we'll look at a good example of transition on the daily chart of the British pound (Ch 17.6). The chart shows a steep trend going into mid-July. By early to mid-August we see that the Wave was broken to the downside thus ending the uptrend. The price action that follows shows how powerful an analytical tool the Wave can be. Notice how it is no longer trending between 12 o'clock and 2 o'clock?

So by now I hope you understand how I conduct my "prep work." It will take some time to train your eyes to find the "best" market environment, and believe me, its well worth the time and effort. With some practice, it will soon become automatic. Once we find a time frame that climbs smoothly with the Wave and retraces back into the Wave, then we have a potential swing trade set up. If we have a time frame that shows a choppy market that does not obey the Wave or show a Wave traveling at three o'clock, we have a potential momentum trading set up. Once we know which set up we are most likely working with, we can begin to draw trendlines, measure recent major rallies or declines with Fibonacci levels, and to confirm and build our trade.

CHAPTER 18

Three Classic Tools to a Three-Step Setup

Three Classic Tools to a Three-Step Setup

If a trader spends a few weekends reading some of the trading books from the early 1900s (specifically books by Richard D. Wyckoff and Richard W. Schabacker), it is eye-opening to see that even though we have the technology of today—computers, the Internet, instant quotes and charts—the nature of the market has changed very little, if at all.

And that's because the motives and emotions that rule the market have not changed. Fear and greed rule...and probably always will. Because of this fact, I purposely sought out books written in the early 1900s because the "crutch" of television and computers were not available to these traders. In my opinion, these books focus on price and chart patterns more than books written in the latter part of the century. Price and chart patterns are the most direct way to measure market emotion.

Analyzing price and chart action using the "classic" tools is a tried and true formula. That's not to say indicators are not powerful assets—you know that I use a set of Moving Averages, aka the "Wave,"

as well as the Commodity Channel Index (CCI) to add depth to my analysis. Let's focus on the three tools that start my analysis of any market: Trendlines, support and resistance lines, minor highs and lows, and Fibonacci levels.

While what we are about to discuss will show how a three-step setup works in the Forex market, it can and does work on everything from stocks to E-Minis, intraday, and end-of-day. Remember that your trading style will dictate how you will use each of these tools for your entry strategy. Many times after you analyze the chart, you will see that one style is better suited than another in the current market environment. For example, because the market is already trading in an established trend, you may focus on swing trading. Perhaps you missed a momentum trade; in that case the three-step analysis will help you set up a swing trade.

Let's begin. First, if you haven't done your prep work please go back and do it! If you have already, great! Step one is drawing major and minor trendlines.

Chart 18.1

Many first-time traders enter positions without respecting the support and resistance of major and minor trendlines. Knowing where the trend is heading is a simple but key point that can begin with the Wave, but eventually you and I must draw trendlines, support, and resistance lines to pinpoint the price levels that we will watch.

The trendlines in Ch 18.1 show multiple downtrends. While the major downtrend line is a thicker line, it is important to note the minor downtrends marked by the thin lines. We can also see a horizontal support level. Trendlines, support, and resistance are all related and are all the building blocks of chart patterns. If you find these levels, you will also find any relevant charting patterns

because most, if not all, chart patterns are made up of some combinations of trendlines, support, and resistance levels. The next step is to locate the "swings" by finding the minor high and low patterns on the chart (Ch 18.2).

Minor highs and minors lows are helpful because they are an easy way of identifying the swings in the market. (See Chap. 10, Fibonacci Levels.) Our goal is to find an accurate way to methodically locate the most recent and relevant swing high and swing low from which we can draw Fibonacci levels. Drawing the Fibonacci levels is step three.

Since we know how to locate the minor highs and minor lows on the chart, we can accurately draw the most relevant Fibonacci retracements and extensions (Ch 18.3). The result is a set of levels that will offer support and resistance until the next major rally or decline. The analysis shows us that the 0.618 and .786 Fibonacci level acted as resistance. The 1.000 level was briefly support before prices fell through the 1.272 and 1.618 levels. While the 1.886 level wasn't hit, prices did stop just above it. The most recent few candles show that the 1.618 level is currently resistance.

Chart 18.2

Each one of these steps unveils an important piece of the analysis puzzle. Trendlines without Fibonacci levels would only show the trend yet would not reveal all relevant support and resistance levels. Fibonacci levels without trendlines would not show potential trendline breaks and the current strength or weakness of the market. Putting these two tools together yields the two most important facets of

any trade: where to enter and where to exit. Everything outside of those two facts is extraneous regardless of whether you are momentum or swing trading. For example, if you were to be swayed

Chart 18.3

by a particular piece of news that changed your bias, that in itself is not wrong but ask yourself these questions: Does the news tell me at what price to enter or exit? You will find that it seldom does because there is no way of calculating what the reaction will be. Instead, consider these questions: Did the release of this news effect price action in a way that prices reached my profit objective or stop-loss? Did it trigger my entry price? Did the news affect the current trend?

If traders want to know if a trend is weakening, they need only to see if the Wave is flattening out. Of course, the most obvious sign would be a trendline break. If traders want to know where to take profits or even where to potentially place a stop-loss, they can use Fibonacci levels and "psychological" or rounds numbers. Psychological numbers are simply whole or round numbers. Limit orders, especially, tend to be placed at numbers ending in 0, for example, 1.2200 or 115.50. Orders congregate at these levels, creating support and resistance. It is for this reason that when one of my entry or exit prices is

close to a psychological level, I will check to see whether my order will be sitting above or below it. The reason is because the support or resistance created by the psychological level could effect my order execution.

If we zoom out to the 60- minute chart, we can see the same downtrend lines that were plotted on the 240-minute chart; however, we can also see a new resistance level just above 1.1950 (Chart 18.4). What is important to note is that as you move from longer time frames to shorter ones, you will often see short-term levels that can set up breakouts and breakdowns.

If we zoom out to the daily chart, we can see a congestion pattern forming, in this case a pennant, which is a triangular

Chart 18.4

pattern that consists of a downtrend and uptrend line that are either about to or actually intersecting (Ch 18.5).

The power of watching multiple time frames, in this case the 60, 240, and daily charts, can open up the possibilities of many trading setups thus giving us the choice of picking the setup that suits our risk tolerances and trading style best. Just remember that eve though each chart is analyzed with the same tools and same methodology, each is treated individually as a trade in its own right. The key to trading success is analysis using tried and true tools and a consistent approach, and now we know how we can choose which

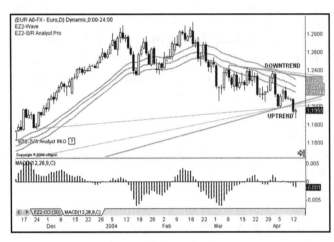

Chart 18.5

setup will suit us best. Again, there is no such thing as the "right" trade. The best thing we can do is choose which trading style is appropriate for the current market environment (i.e., swing versus momentum). Now that we have a broad overview of the three classic steps, let's get an in-depth look at each one.

CHAPTER 19

Building a Trade

Building a Trade

I have a philosophy when it comes to consistency in my trade: recognize, react, repeat. Those are my three Rs. That's the backbone of building a trade.

We want to use the same steps so that we can analyze the market without emotion and without getting too caught up in the moment. The key is consistency. We want a consistent plan to enter a trade and set profit targets and stop-loss levels. Having a methodology is important to success because without a plan to follow, we will be open to outside influences, which is something that I sadly see too often when I see other traders...new and experienced!

Building a trade means just that: We will follow a blueprint in the expectation that we can and will produce a repeatable result. Our final product is a successful trade. Though "success" is not just simply defined as a profitable trade, as many traders would think. A successful trade is one that is built, using price and chart action, with a specific entry, profit targets, and stop-loss. Even if the trade gets stopped out, believe me that is still success! It means that you were following the plan. The worst, most dangerous trade anyone can make is one that breaks the rules—like chasing a trade or not adhering to the stop-loss—and still makes a profit! This alone has been the demise of many a trader in the long run because there is always the temptation that if we got away with it once, we can get away with it again. You've chosen to read this book to learn a skill, perhaps even build a new or second career. Learning these next three steps is the first step in the right direction.

Throughout the years, I have traded many markets, intraday and end-of-day: Stocks, futures, and Forex. The blueprint I am teaching you will work on any market and any time frame because it's not some new trick or secret indicator. It is the culmination of three time-tested classic tools that rely on price action and the natural ebb and flow of the market to dictate where and when to enter and exit the market.

Step One of Building a Trade: Draw Your Trendlines

The first step is to locate the trendlines on the chart. I recommend you look at a lot of charts so that you may begin to train your eyes to notice the lines (trendlines) and levels (horizontal support and resistance) that make up a trend and any chart patterns. Practice makes perfect. Since we have completed the prep work that precedes any trade setup, we have a good idea of the direction and strength of the trend based upon what the Wave has indicated. Drawing lines and levels allows us to see the specific prices that we will watch to enter and manage our trade. (See Chap. 8, How to Draw Trendlines.) Don't forget that we are looking for both major and minor trendlines.

In this chart of the euro on a daily time frame we see that there are two downtrend lines, one major and one minor (Ch 19.1). Notice the support level, which as we

know represents buyers. This chart shows us two things. First, the market is in a downtrend. Second, and more important, there is a strong support level that is the floor of a consolidation pattern. Consolidation means that we are seeing the trend flatten out and a range form. Since the beginning of May you can see that prices are more choppy than in a downtrend. You can call it a trading range or a rectangle pattern but the bottom line is that it is best to wait for a breakout/breakdown and set up a momentum trade.

The next chart of the British pound shows a total of three trendlines (Ch 19.2). The trendlines are forming a triangle or pennant, which is a consolidation pattern.

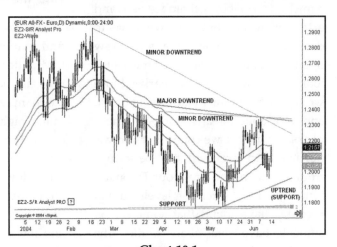

Chart 19.1

The first thought that should run through your mind is that there is no dominant trend. The second thought is that entering the market before a trend reveals itself (by a breakout/breakdown) would be a low percentage trade. However, this is a great chart to keep an eye on since we can wait for this momentum trade to set up and confirm.

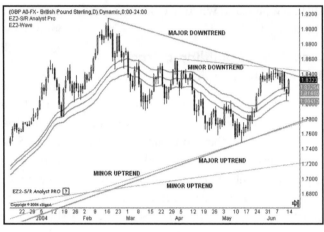

Chart 19.2

While trendlines alone seem to be giving us a lot of insight into any trade setups we may want to take, we can do even more to set up and confirm a trade, namely, draw Fibonacci retracement and extension levels. But first we have to determine from where we will draw them, and you now know that means we look for the swings in the market. Since we have drawn our trendlines, support, and resistance already, some of those peaks and valleys we connected to draw our lines and levels will also be swings from which we can draw our Fibonacci retracement and extension levels. In that regard, I have found that some of my students have gone about finding the swings in the market before drawing their lines and levels, and that's perfectly

acceptable. You can certainly try that and see if it helps.

Step Two of Building a Trade: Find the Swings in the Market

We are already familiar with how to find swings with minor high and minor low patterns. While actual swings are typically calculated from a percentage-based move rather than a pattern like minor highs and lows, and you can use either. Typically I will initially teach new traders how to find minor highs and minor lows because they are simple patterns that are easy to recognize until your eyes are trained to find actual high and low swings by just glancing at the chart. And believe me, there will be a time when most of these patterns, trendlines, levels, support, and resistance will just seem to pop out from the chart.

Swings are commonly calculated by a percentage move. So if we choose a percentage move of 5% for example, then prices must move up at least 5% from a low for it to become a confirmed swing low. It's just the opposite for swing highs. Since this is more mathematical, and you certainly don't want to get bogged down in calculating this for each swing, let's move on to minor high and lows.

Let's briefly review some charting examples. The first chart example is of the euro on a 180-minute time frame and shows quite a few minor highs and minor lows (Ch 19.3). As traders it is our job to take these patterns and decide which we feel is the most timely and relevant. Remember, in order to draw the most accurate Fibonacci levels as possible, we want to find what would best be described as the "last major move."

The move from *a* to *b* is not a consideration because it is obviously not a major move (Chart 19.3). The move from *c* to

d is certainly a good option and at the time would have been a good choice. Finally we have the most recent move from *e* to *f* or from *e* to *g*. Since *g* is higher than *f* it would be a better choice since there was not a significant retracement between *f* and *g*. Let's examine the move from *e* to *g* and determine whether it is indeed the last major move.

The move from *e* to *g* is the last or most recent move, so the first criterion is met. But the most important criteria is whether it is the major move. There are two questions to ask when we seek to qualify what is a major move:

Question 1.

Is there a swing higher or lower than the swings (or minor high/minor low) that

Chart 19.3

we're looking at, AND has there been any significant retracement at, all between those two points? In this case, we can answer no. There is no minor low that is lower than *e* and no minor high that is higher than *g* and the market has not retraced significantly between these two points. It is vital that the last major move be a

Chart 19.4

rally or sell-off that has not already been retraced. That is the reason we would not consider a move from *c* to *e* because there was a retracement in between these two points.

Question 2.

Are the swings (or minor) high and low too close together? In this case, no. When the swings are too close together, the market cannot rally or sell off enough between the two points to offer a retracement. In this example, the market had moved from around 1.1950 to 1.2100, which is 150 pips, which offered a good range.

So we can now see that the move from *e* to *g* has satisfied the two criteria we can use to decide whether the move we are

looking at is the last major move. Let's look at another example, this time the Canadian dollar on a daily chart (Ch 19.4).

I've marked the last two minor highs with *a* and *b* and the minor low with *c*. The question here is whether to use the move from *a* to *c* or from *b* to *c*. I chose this example for a purpose. It shows that there is no absolute when picking the "right" last major move. Some traders may feel that *a* to *c* would be the right move, while others would say that there was enough retracement to nullify the move. Others would say then that the move from *b* to *c* is the right one since it traveled far enough and had no retracement in between. The argument against the move from *b* to *c* would be that there is a higher swing/minor high than the *b* level. So which is it?

Frankly, both would do. Your answer to question 1 would determine which to use. And there really is no "right" answer as long as the two criteria are met. In these situations I recommend drawing the Fibonacci levels from both levels. Many times when you do this you will see that certain levels will overlap with trendlines, support, and resistance, psychological or round numbers. I've said it before and I'll say it again: Practice makes perfect. So let's get to step three: drawing Fibonacci levels.

Step Three: Drawing Fibonacci Levels

Even though step three is focused on drawing Fibonacci levels, it is truly the step that ties all our other prep work and analysis together to give us a clear picture of any set up. This means that during this step we will be deciding upon a potential entry, profit targets, and stop-loss. And we know that our underlying thought under all this is the three "Rs": recognize, react, repeat.

The goal of any trader is to "train your eyes" in order to recognize the lines and levels that make up a trade set up. Fibonacci levels have different roles in your trading depending upon the type of trade you are setting up. For momentum trades, Fibonacci levels act as secondary confirmation, stop-loss levels, and profit targets. For swing traders, Fibonacci levels act as entry levels and profit targets. The Fibonacci levels also act as stop-loss levels for swing trades as well. Often in swing trades the entry price and stop loss will be the same level because we are buying pullbacks in an uptrend or shorting resistance in a downtrend. As long as prices do not trade beyond our entry price, our trade is valid. Of course, because of this close proximity between entry level and stop-loss, we want to give the market a little room to move or wiggle. We can also use any available support or resistance levels that we feel will contain prices, and this includes psychological or round numbers.

Alternately, when swing trading with pullbacks or bounces to the Wave we can use a different stop-loss strategy. The Wave is made up of three moving average lines. If, for example, we get a pullback into the middle line of the Wave (which means we're trading with an uptrend), we can use a break below the bottom line of the Wave as a stop-loss. We would simply place out stop between 5 and 10 pips below the bottom line of the Wave.

If we were trading with a downtrend and prices bounced into the bottom line of the Wave, we can use either the middle or top line as our stop-loss. If prices bounce into the top line of a downtrend or pullback into the bottom line in an uptrend, we simply use that line as the stop-loss with a 5 to 10 pip wiggle.

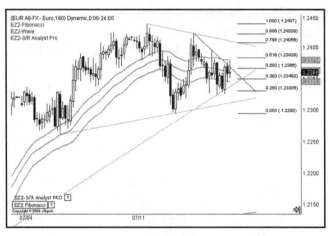

Chart 19.5

Let's focus on the two set ups you will use the most: momentum and swing. We will discuss a momentum trade set up first. For momentum trades we are looking for a trendline, support, or resistance to be broken. The Fibonacci level from the last major move can serve as confirmation; however, this is not a necessity to trade entry.

In this example of the euro on the 180-minute chart we see a potential downtrend line breakout with the 50% Fibonacci level acting as secondary confirmation (Ch 19.5). We also see an uptrend line with support levels at the 0.382 and 0.500 Fibonacci levels. These lines form a triangle or pennant formation with a three o'clock Wave. This kind of confirmation is exactly what we like to see. Because this is a momentum trade, we can take the uptrend line breakdown or downtrend line breakout. By the way, I am all the more confident of a predicable follow-through when I see a Fibonacci level acting as secondary confirmation like that of the potential downtrend line breakout. I have a high-probability breakout/breakdown level when I have a trendline, support, or resistance plus the Fibonacci level at the same price area. This is because there are actually two reasons to take the trade. Multiple reasons mean that there are more traders watching a move because there is increased attention being paid to this price level and more participation equals a better follow-through!

Another set of lines I want to bring to your attention are the second and third uptrend lines lower on the chart. Both will be support levels and potential profit targets if we take the highest uptrend line breakdown. If we do not take the first breakdown, we can see if the second or third level will set up a momentum trade. The same applies to a potential breakout regarding the second downtrend line higher on the chart.

For swing trades we will rely on pullbacks (or bounces) to enter a trade. As we have discussed before, these pullbacks will typically be to Fibonacci levels or the Wave. Unlike momentum trades where we will rely on breakouts and breakdowns, swing trading setups will not always offer us any trendlines from which to buy or short. However, we are trading retracements, and those are indeed support and resistance levels! Support is created by buyers, so when an uptrend pulls back to a level that we have analyzed is support, there is a high probability that prices will remain above this area or bounce off from there. Resistance is created by sellers, so when a downtrend bounces up to a resistance level, we expect prices to reverse at or stay below this level. There a few questions a trader asks when they are swing trading:

1. What is the prevailing trend? (If any?)
2. Where are the support levels for an ptrend entry? or Where are the resistance levels for a downtrend entry? (Whichever applies to the current trend.)
3. Is Wave traveling at Chris Clock Angles?

When we trade swing setups we must understand that if prices break the down through the pullback level or break up through the bounce level that the trade is no longer valid as your stop-loss will most likely be hit. However, I recommend giving prices a little wiggleroom at these support and resistance levels. It's best to figure in the typical five-pip spread and psychological or round numbers. By giving your swing trade stop-loss levels this wiggle, you are less likely to get stopped out by the daily fluctuation these support and resistance levels can experience and still maintain a valid trade.

CHAPTER 20

Rewriting Trade Management

Rewriting Trade Management

The Forex market, because of it's sheer mass and participation adheres very well to charting and technical analysis. It is for this very reason that traders would do well to focus their set ups and trade management to the charts rather than news and fundamentals.

Remember our mantra: If an analysis tool doesn't show us at what price to get in or get out...we shouldn't use it!

This end-of-day chart of the EUR/USD has two tools active on the chart: trendlines and Fibonacci levels (Ch 20.1). These time-tested, classic tools answer the three questions I ask myself when I am entering and managing a trade: where to enter, where to place my stop-loss, and where are my profit targets.

On May 3, the market consolidated (Ch 20.2). When that happens you know what we do, right? We wait for a breakout to the upside or a breakdown to the downside. The chart shows that we have a major uptrend to break as well as another support level and a major downtrend to break as well as the 0.382 Fibonacci level. All chart patterns boil down to support and resistance, and that includes downtrend and

Chart 20.1

uptrends which in this example have formed a triangle.

On May 5 we see that the market broke out to the upside and traded through the first profit target at the 0.500 Fibonacci level and the second profit target at 0.618, and stalled just above the 1.21487 price level (Ch 20.3). Each of these Fibonacci resistance levels becomes support as prices trade up through them and can effectively be used as trailing stops if prices reverse. The 0.618 can now be seen as a support level and a near term trailing stop. Be sure to give it a 5 to 10 pip wiggle. We could also use the 0.500 level as a stop-loss level, but this depends upon how much profit you are willing to give back to the market. Both the 0.618 and 0.5000 levels are viable options. Personally, I am not wild about the idea of giving back 70-plus pips. But again, it's your decision.

Chart 20.2

As we see here (Ch 20.4), prices did weaken and we see that the 0.618 level was indeed the reversal level and prices have broken the 0.500 Fibonacci level, thus closing out the long position.

Chart 20.3

The next chart shows the view as of May 10. The EUR/USD has continued to sell off, and a large consolidation pattern (a downtrend and uptrend trying to converge) has begun to develop (Ch 20.5). Since we have a new last major move we are looking at a new set of Fibonacci levels. Remember, we must continually monitor rallies and declines to be sure that we have the most recent and relevant Fibonacci levels. Prices are currently trading at the 0.786 Fibonacci level and had already bounced off the 0.886 level earlier. Having these levels on the chart helps a trader gauge the strength of the market as well as have potential support and resistance levels laid out on the chart.

Confirmation of a potential break of the uptrend line would coincide with the 0.886 Fibonacci level. There is also a horizontal support level at the 1.000 (full retrace-

Chart 20.4

ment) level which is also support in itself. This support level (with secondary confirmation) would be the first potential profit target level if prices break down below our entry level at the 0.886

Chart 20.5

level. Let's rewind and take a look at this set-up on an intraday chart (Ch 20.6).

The intraday view is of the 180-minute chart. Here we see prices resting right on the uptrend line. To the upside we see a minor resistance level not far above the 0.618 Fibonacci level. The uptrend line and the minor or soft resistance level are forming two breakout levels that we will watch closely. I will refer to a support or resistance level as *soft* when it is not perfectly horizontal, which means that the prices connected to make the level were not at the same price. If the prices are very close or at the same price level and make a perfectly horizontal support or resistance level, I will refer to it as *firm*.

Here's the view seven candles later: Prices broke the uptrend lines and the sell-off sliced down through the first profit target at the 0.786 Fibonacci level and

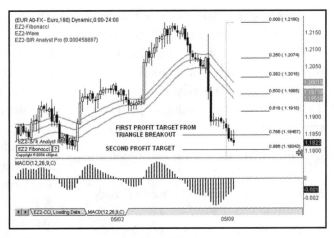

Chart 20.6

headed toward the second target at the 0.886 (Ch 20.7). The next chart is just four candles later and shows a great example of when prices fall short of a target and what can happen.

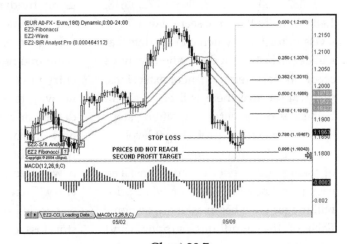

Chart 20.7

Here we see that the low reached 1.1807 while the profit target was 1.1804...three lousy pips, but that's the way trading can go (Ch 19.8). Since we have the 0.786 Fibonacci level just above, it makes for a perfect trailing stop. In this scenario, our Fibonacci levels acted as

1. A potential stop-loss at the onset of the triangle break
2. The initial profit target once the break confirmed
3. A trailing stop when the second profit target was not hit

By using Fibonacci, traders can use the levels to confirm entries as well as exits. There are a number of Fibonacci retracement and extension levels that can be used; however, I personally use these: .250, .382, .500, .618, .786, .886, 1.272, 1.618, 1.886. Initially this may seem like a lot of levels to track but when considering that a trade can be triggered anywhere within a set of Fibonacci retracement or extensions, you will see that there will be levels on both sides of the entry pinpointing stop-loss levels as well as profit target levels.

Remember that trading is the process of asking and answering questions. The trick is in knowing when or what price will trigger us to begin asking questions. Each of the trendlines, support, and resistance levels on a chart can be consid-

ered "decision levels," because when prices reach these levels we should begin asking ourselves: Will prices breakout or breakdown here? Will prices reverse here? Will prices level and find support or resistance here? Decision levels keep us from asking questions at the wrong price levels, and they also allow us to relax because each new bar or candle doesn't create an anxiety that makes us feel that we should be "doing" something. This is especially true for short-term intraday traders because prices are constantly moving and changing.

Chartists and technical traders rely on price and chart patterns because fundamentals and news cannot give a trader exact price levels at which to buy and sell. One error some traders make is using fundamentals alone to trigger a trade. While a trader has the option of timing an entry with the release of an economic report, if they already have a entry price set by the charts, there still is no way to accurately measure to what degree any piece of news has already been discounted into the market. Since we cannot gauge the reaction to this news event, this results in a high-risk entry. There is simply no way to generate a specific price at which to enter, place a stop-loss, or profit target based solely on fundamentals or news.

One of most common ways many traders decide upon stop-loss levels is to use a fixed point or percentage based stop-loss. This no doubt has come from the influence the money-management style from large funds and portfolios have had on trading. The error in this is that traders are neither creating portfolios nor investing. As we have discussed in Chap. 13, Trading Versus Investing, trading is a completely separate activity which has its own rules. Most commonly, traders will enter a trade based upon some sort of action at a specific price point, whether that trigger is a pullback, bounce, breakdown, or breakout. Our entries are triggered by price, so should our exits. Exits can be stop-loss or profit targets.

As I've shown here, by using Fibonacci to manage the trade, a trader does not have to use fixed points or percentages to decide upon stop-loss or profit targets. Besides, we know that the market neither acknowledges nor cares that a trader may only tolerate a 2% or 4 points of loss or that he or she is setting a profit target for $400 or 10 points. These fixed points have no basis within the market.

Think about it this way: Chartists and technical traders believe that by monitoring price action and price patterns they can formulate a trade, specifically an entry. However, far too many of these same traders seem to abandon this belief in price and patterns when deciding upon stop-losses and profit targets which suddenly seem to be based on a dollar value. (e.g.. "I want to make $500 on this trade and only want to risk $100.") This is completely without merit! When in a long trade, we should be looking to support levels below our entry price as potential stop-loss levels and if we are in a short trade we should be looking to a resistance level above our entry for stop-loss levels.

Even when using the charts, there is no one "right" price to place a stop-loss. This decision also depends on the rules a trader uses to qualify or disqualify a trade based upon whether the trade is a momentum or swing trade. Some traders have deeper pockets and use longer time frames which results in a different risk tolerance than a trader with less capital and a shorter time frame. The charts offer flexibility and the ability to decide—before entering the trade—what the stop-loss and initial profit target is. And by using the charts, these decisions are not made arbitrarily! Instead, we can now plan ahead and decide upon these levels by using Fibonacci levels, support, and resistance levels.

CHAPTER 21

A Trade
Going Astray

A Trade Going Astray

Fellow Traders,
This is my letter to you. Once upon a time, like you, I began this journey of learning how to trade. I wanted to learn to do it well and quickly. And like you, well maybe some of you, it became an all-out obsession. Do 14-hour days in front of the PC sound familiar?

That was me. A great weekend was lying out by my pool or at the beach with a book on charting or technical analysis.

As I continued on my relentless pursuit of reading and watching whatever I could get my hands on, I discovered all those books, courses, videos, and websites that told me that *they* had the "secret" and that *they* caught all the turns, tops, bottoms. When you are looking for an edge, the "holy grail of trading" song calls to you. What you don't know is that there are already so many traders that were called by the same song and wrecked their ships on the rocks. (Forgive my Ulysses and the sirens analogy, it's the English major in me). There is a fact that when I accepted it, it became the turning point in my trading, and it is this: Not all market moves are mine to profit from. Not every move is for me. A move that makes money for one trader will be a loss for another or won't even register a setup for yet another. *That's the real secret.*

As I think back, it really was a pivotal moment in my trading education because once I accepted this fact I stopped my "search." I stopped looking for why my way didn't make money when I read on a forum or saw on a chat that someone else made money. I stopped trying to figure out why I couldn't capture every move and why some moves left me behind. *I know why now: Not every move is for me.*

So I became patient and learned what it meant when great traders say "let the trade come to you." Wise words, but tough to understand until you believe that "not every move is for me." Accepting that my approach of using "classic" tools like trendlines, support, resistance, and Fibonacci had their limitations was step one. *Say it aloud: "My trading approach has limitations."* The fact is that no single approach can capture every move of the market. Every approach has environments in which it is properly designed and suited for. Every trading approach has limitations.

Analysis and trading should be methodical so that you follow the same mindset with each and every trade, like a great recipe you know will always come out right. A lot of you may already know this, so let's talk about when a trade doesn't work as planned. We all know it happens. There is not a system, approach, method, or strategy on Earth that will work 100% of the time. However I believe that when a trader follows his or her rules and knows when to swing versus momen-

tum trade, the chance of coming out of the trade poorly is far less. There's only one thing worse than following your rules and losing, and that's breaking your rules and winning! Think about it.

So let's look at the anatomy of a trade when you follow your rules and the trade doesn't work out as planned. This chart shows a breakout above two key levels (Ch 21.1).

First was the resistance at the 0.382 Fibonacci level at 1.2135. This level had five tests and is firm resistance. The second level is the top line of the Wave with the CCI at over +100. (See Chap. 12, Measuring Trends with CCI on Short- and Long-Term Charts.)

Remember that the Wave is a visual tool that acts as a cue to trend and

Chart 21.1

momentum as well as support and resistance. While it is not a rule, rather a preference, I find that many times it is better to see a close through a breakout/breakdown level. In this case we see the close above both the 0.382 and Wave with the current candle.

If we fast-forward three candles from the first chart, we see another confirmation of the trend with the close above the next resistance level of this uptrend, and that is the 0.500 Fibonacci level (Ch 21.2). This level would be the first opportunity to take part of the position off the table. In other words, you downsize your overall position here. Smart traders get out when they can, not when they have to. This level was the first potential resistance and should be the first level a trader should take profits at. I prefer to "peel out" of my position one or two lots at a time. I prefer to buy in pairs: two lot, four lot, etc., at my initial entry level. An easy trick to deciding how many lots to enter with is to count how many potential profit targets you have. Sometimes that number may only be two

or three—sometimes it will be six or eight. I never pillar or pyramid because if the trade moves against me, as I add lots to my position, it will become "top heavy." (Pillaring or pyramiding is a way to add to your position as a trade moves in your favor, typically as your make enough profits to justify another lot.) If and when the market reverses, you lose your profits at a greater velocity than at which you made them. With this in mind, the next profit level as is the 0.618 level. We also see that we have an uptrend line, which strengthens the chance of the trend continuing further.

Fast forward one candle and we see that the days candle topped out just below the 0.618 level, which is set to be our second profit taking level (Ch 21.3). The 0.500

Chart 21.2

level did act as support and we would take this as a positive sign because what was once support and is now resistance. When a price level is tested as both support and resistance, it reinforces the fact that this level is important to both the bulls and the bears.

Are there exceptions to when a chartist may look to the fundamentals like reports and news? Certainly, while news does not help answer the only two questions in trading—which you should know by heart—it is helpful to know when reports are going to be released or if there are large scheduled events that are shaping trader opinion. For the purposes of this example, ignore any underlying fundamentals that may have been applicable. So that brings us to the next chart (Ch 21.4).

I'm not going to try and spin this at all...the market took a nose dive, plain and simple. So let's discuss our stop-loss.

Chart 21.3

Here's what we do when a trade doesn't work as planned. There are a number of support levels that traders of any risk tolerance can utilize. You already know that I do not believe in using a set number of

Chart 21.4

pips, ticks, points, or a percentage for a stop loss. If the price action levels trigger an entry, then price action levels should trigger the stop and profit targets.

The next profit target we were waiting on was the 0.618 level at 1.2232 since we had just traded up through the 0.500 level at 1.2184. If what was once resistance is now support then the closest stop loss would be a breakdown through the 0.500 level. For traders who would like to give the market more wiggle room, they could use the top line of the Wave.

Considering that as this market traded sharply lower, stopping the long trade out…there are some support levels that can also trigger shorts. The uptrend line and the 0.382 are at the same level, and that's secondary confirmation. For a Wave/CCI combo set up to trigger an entry prices would have to trade through the bottom line of the Wave *and* register at least a −100 CCI reading, which we do not have.

When a trader knows the tools there are always a number of things he or she can choose from to manage the trade. This is why it is so important

to have a methodical way to analyze the markets with tools that are consistent. I am not going to suddenly introduce a slow stochastic or a MACD divergence or an RSI into the trade. While they may be great tools for another trader, they simply are not part of the consistent tools I have chosen. Be watchful of trading inconsistencies that are a direct result of using too many or unfamiliar tools! Keep the tools familiar, simple, and consistent.

How important is it to obey the stop-loss and not become "gun shy" after a loss? ("Gun shy" refers to traders that will hesitate to take valid trading setups after a loss.)

Take a look at the chart as it stands now (Chart 21.5). The highlighted area is the area shows the sharp sell-off that

Chart 21.5

took us out of the long trade. You can see now how much lower prices are trading. Even if the short trade wasn't taken...it is vital that traders heed the warnings on a chart and get out when their stop-loss is hit. We had two if not three chart validated stop loss levels. There was a chance to get out and more than enough reasons to do so.

We know that one underlying mindset for entries and exits is knowing your "ands" and "ors." When entering the market the reasoning works with "ands": *"X must happen and Y and Z."* When exiting the market, however it is a bit different as the mindset should be guided by "or": *"If A happens or B happens or C happens, then I'm out!"* I know not every trade is going to go in my favor. Frankly I've seen traders who break their rules and make a lot of money...for a short while. Inevitably they will lose and lose bigger than they won. *You know it's true because either you've experienced it or know someone who has.* Staying in this trading game is about managing risk and conserving capital. The old saying it true: Trading is not a sprint, it's a marathon.

CHAPTER 22

Placing Your Orders

Placing Your Orders

Placing orders is one of the most misunderstood aspects of trading. Before I began writing this book, I spoke with fellow and would-be traders about what they'd like to see in the book, and one of the most common requests was for information and instruction on placing orders.

So let's begin to simplify. Forget all those fancy definitions, and let's get straight to what you will be using day in and day out when you are trading. In my opinion, there are only two orders you need to concern yourself with: limit orders and stop (or stop-loss) orders.

Most orders are going to revolve around three actions: how to get into the market, how to exit the market, and how to protect yourself when you are away from your computer. The orders that you will use are not complicated. Most order entry platforms will show you two quotes for each pair. In this example of the EUR/USD we see that we can buy at 1.2211 and sell at 1.2215. This means that there is a four-pip (price interest point or the smallest price increment) spread.

Since we are placing an order at a specific price and we do not want a fill worse than this price, we are placing a limit order. (For those of you out there that would like to know the main difference between Limit and Market Orders, when you place a market order, you cannot specify price!) When you have placed a limit order you have made two things clear:

EUR/USD	
Sell	Buy
1.22	1.22
11	**15**
Low	High
1.2211	1.2215

1. You want to enter at a specific price.
2. You will not accept a fill higher than you limit order to buy or lower than you limit order to sell.

Because we pay the spread when trading Forex, our buy orders will be filled at the ask or offer, and our sell orders will be filled at the bid. Remember that the bid is made up of all the people who are willing to buy for a certain price, and the ask are all the sellers that will sell for a certain price. It's the difference in price between the two groups that makes up the spread. After all, sellers always want to sell at the highest price they can, and buyers always want to buy at the lowest price they can. The prices that we see on our order entry platform represents the best bid and ask that we can execute at that time through our broker. Here is an example of what we may see at any given time on a number of pairs.

These all represent limit orders. When the quoted price meets our entry price, it's as easy as a mouse click. Our next task is entering the stop or stop-loss order. While order entry platforms vary, most systems will allow you to enter your stop price when you place your entry order or as a contingent order just after you enter. For example, we can click on the Stop column (see the Open Positions image) and enter our stop-loss order. I am not going to get into platform specifics here because there are nuances to each but let's talk about the mechanics of a stop-loss.

EUR/USD		USD/JPY		GBP/USD		USD/CHF	
Sell	Buy	Sell	Buy	Sell	Buy	Sell	Buy
1.22	1.22	110	110	1.83	1.83	1.25	1.25
11	**15**	**24**	**29**	**35**	**40**	**26**	**31**
Low	High	Low	High	Low	High	Low	High
1.2211	1.2215	110.24	110.29	1.8335	1.8340	1.2526	1.2531

A stop-loss is really an interesting hybrid of a limit and market order in that it uses elements of each. First, we can specify a price at which to place our stop-loss. However, when this price is met, the order turns into a market order, getting us out of the market at the next market price. So we are *guaranteed* the exit unlike a limit order. Limit orders specify that we will only accept a fill at or better the price we specify.

Now let's get into some avanced concepts, namely understaing how the spread effects your fill. Since pre-planning theselimit and stop orders involve some preemptive action, let's take a moment to talk about execution. Remember since we pay the "spread" in Forex we're usually dealing with about a three to five pip difference between the bid and the ask. This means we have to think about where our order will be executed. It is best to figure in the spread into your order because your order represents a price on the chart without consideration of the spread. Remember that sell stops are filled on our bid, and buy stops are filled on our offer.

Here's a simple rule: buyers are support and sellers a resistance. So here's your rule of thumb: For entries that are breakouts, which mean that the entry relies on a trade up through a resistance level, I will add five pips to the entry price so that when I enter the trade, the bid is trading at the breakout level and is thus support. This means that my entry will be five pips above the breakout level price.

For breakdowns my entry relies on a trade down through a support level. I will subtract five pips to the entry price so that when I enter the trade, the offer is trading at the breakdown level and is now resistance. Let's look at some a charting example (Chart 22.1).

The two arrows on the chart point to a potential breakout and a potential breakdown that could occur on this intraday chart of the British pound. There are some real-world decisions that we must make. All the levels on a chart are fine and good, but first things first: We have to make some determinations about at what price we will enter. We see that there are three downtrends close together around the breakout area. *So which one do we take?* Aggressive traders can take the initial breakout level, which is the

one closest to current prices. More conservative traders can take the level furthest away from current prices. Realize that there is no absolute here. If you take the aggressive entry, you may be prone to false breakouts. Take the conservative entry, and you will be adding to your risk because your stop-loss will be further from your entry. *Think back to the risk/reward ratio.*

A factor that can influence the strength of a breakout or breakdown level is whether there is any kind of support or resistance confirmation at that level. This could be a horizontal support or resistance line or Fibonacci retracement or extension. When you look at both the breakout and breakdown level on the British pound chart you can see

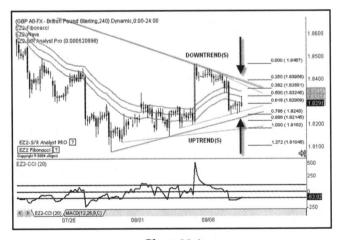

Chart 22.1

that there is the 0.250 Fibonacci level just above the downtrend line and the 0.618 level just below the uptrend line. The confirmation of breaking through two chart levels at the same or close to the same price is certainly more powerful that breaking through just one. Consider that the breakout level on the British pound has two trendlines and the 0.250 Fibonacci retracement in close proximity. Compared to the single downtrend line, which would be an aggressive breakout, this higher "more conservative" level is a better choice since it has more significant price action. When we look at the uptrend lines, we notice that the three lines are not in close proximity to one another. In this case the highest of the breakdown levels also has the 0.618 Fibonacci retracement level acting as support. This is the better of the three uptrend lines because of this.

Another decision we must make hinges upon whether we will simply wait for a trade through our price or whether we will wait for a close through our price. Again, there is no right or wrong answer, but there are compromises to be made. If we trade based upon a "pierce" (simply a trade through our price and not a close through), we will experience times when the trade does not follow through. If we wait for a close we can experience slippage from our desired breakout price as compared to the actual close. *And we still haven't any guarantee of a follow-through.* This is why it is vital to have a stop-loss to protect ourselves from trades that do not follow through.

One tool I have found that has been useful to me to confirm breakouts and breakdowns is the MACD histogram. *I use this indicator in this capacity only; to confirm the trade through a level I am watching.* I want to make that perfectly clear. I first started using the MACD histogram as a confirmation tool when I started trading futures because I wanted a tool to help filter out false breakouts. I then began using the tool intraday in my E-Mini S&P trading and it worked masterfully. I like that the Histogram bars are either above the zero or signal line or they are not. It is an "on/off" indicator. It's no magic bullet, and I will admit that sometimes I will miss an entry because the MACD histogram does not confirm...but I've always believed in the idea that I should look for reasons to *not* take the trade, instead for reasons to take the trade. Here we can see the breakdown that of the same British pound chart confirmed by the MACD histogram (Ch 22.2).

The reason I have not spent any time discussing these factors concerning swing trades is because swing entries are a different matter altogether. A swing trade can be executed at the Wave, which gives us an automatic stop-loss by using either one or two of the Wave's levels or by placing a stop 5 to 10 pips beyond the last Wave. For swing trades executed at Fibonacci retracements and Exten-

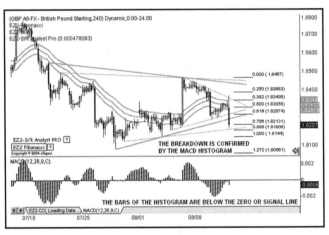

Chart 22.2

sions, we can place a stop 5 to 10 pips beyond the Fibonacci level. In this regard there are no false breakouts or breakdowns to contend with. Either the entry level holds or our stop-loss is hit.

Placing your order is not a complicated process and I encourage you to use demo accounts to learn the ins and outs of the platforms that are available. Most of your trades will be executed via limit and stop orders, and these are not complicated. I would also recommend trying a couple of different platforms to get a feel for the different features that each can offer. Brokerages have people on staff to walk you through every aspect of an order entry platform.

CHAPTER ㉓

The Five Stages of Loss

The Five Stages of Loss

There is no separating trading from psychology. They are forever mixed because when we have our money in the markets, that situation alone will create emotions we will most certainly have to deal with.

It is inevitable! My sister has a PhD in psychology. I bring this up because I am infinitely proud of her, but more important, because she and I have had great debates and discussions about how people behave when their money and ego are on the line.

It's not just the gain or loss of money that effects our emotions. Never underestimate the power of the ego. Ego is attached to the decisions we make. It's our ego that wants us to be right. It's our ego that keeps us from admitting we're wrong. It's amazing how the events and experiences of our life shape the way we trade. Some traders are aggressive or "trigger happy" and have a tendency to overtrade. Others are "gun-shy" and approach each trade too conservatively, even hesitantly. Most of us are somewhere in between with a slight lean toward one side or the other.

It was only after a streak of losing trades very early in my trading career that I finally recognized the psychology of loss. An especially rough week trading the British pound sent me reeling. I was breaking my own rules trying to pick a top in the pound. A group of us traders used to meet at a local cigar shop to talk about the markets—the shop made a great espresso, too. During one of these gatherings I was talking about the pound and one of my trading comrades said, "You're in denial," and proceeded to give me a breakdown of why the pound was going to stay strong. What hit me, though, was his statement that I was in denial. *Was I long because I was bullish, or was I bullish because I was long?* There probably was a time that I bought because my charts showed me reasons to be bullish. But now with the market moving against me, I was rationalizing why I was long, why I should stay long, and why the market was wrong. Long and wrong.

I was in denial. My ego created a scenario that didn't have any basis in reality! Meanwhile, I was still long on the pound, losing money. I returned home and was studying the charts still thinking about my denial when my sister told me of the five stages of loss and that I was in stage one: denial.

The five stages of loss are denial, anger, bargaining, depression, and acceptance. Some of you may already be familiar with this but may not have considered it within the context of trading. I don't mean to be insensitive comparing a trading loss to a loss of life. However, the stages are the same with any loss that we internalize, like a losing trade. The key to understanding each of the five stages of loss is to recognize that we're in it before we let it go to far and get to the final stage of acceptance as soon as possible. So let's briefly discuss each of the stages.

Whenever we are in a trade that is going against us there is going to be denial. It's like a delusional optimism: *It wasn't our action that was wrong; the market is just correcting or digesting pieces of small news.* Whatever the reason we use, it's just a temporary thing that will run its course. We rationalize that this is just a pullback or bounce. We listen and seek out opinions that agree with our positions and ignore those that don't.

Next we move onto anger and this is probably the stage that hits the hardest. Once we run out of reasons to deny that we are wrong, we get angry. We blame a lousy fill, our broker, the charts, our software, the telephone broke our concentration, or an errand kept us from placing a stop-loss. Believe me when I tell you that I have blamed a bad trade on my dogs.

Now that we are angry at everything and everyone, we shift gears. We realize that we're not getting anywhere with being mean and nasty and now decide that being nice might be the best course. We begin bargaining with ourselves, with God, with anyone who will listen, promising that we'll do right next time. The most common bargain is *"If my position comes back to where I got in, I promise I will get out."*

With our family and friends (and pets!) avoiding us, and our bargains unanswered, we sink into stage four: depression. Depression has many physical and psychological symptoms. Traders will notice insomnia, fatigue, lack of focus—especially with anything pertaining to the markets, not talking with friends and family, and refusing help from anyone who wants to help or advises you to exit the position.

Last is acceptance. This is the stage that we want to get to as soon as possible. Acceptance means exiting the position either because the brokerage forced us to or because we finally accepted the situation and took action to fix it. In trading, the outcome is the same: we exit the position. And often it is a "forced acceptance" because the brokerage will liquidate our position. Acceptance is easier and quicker to accomplish if we can recognize the first four steps and come to terms with the losing trade.

A trader doesn't go through the stages in a set way; for example, he or she may slip back from depression into anger. I've observed many traders go back and forth between denial and anger. Interestingly enough, traders will also go through these five stages in a profit situation when they miss a profit target and begin to lose profits from the trade. Even if traders are in a net profitable position, they still feel the pain of giving back those profits and will begin going through the stages of loss, many times giving back their entire profit from the trade.

Want to know a losing trader's famous last words? *"I can't get out now— I'm losing too much!"*

CHAPTER 24

Tips and Tricks of the Trade

Tips and Tricks of the Trade

There are lessons that I have learned over the years: The tips that I have picked up from trading the markets and the tricks from other traders kind enough to want to help a young kid out when she was first starting to trade. I think they will help you so I'm going to take some time right now to do a "brain dump" and share with you a couple of tips that have kept me out of trouble and tricks that have made my trading life more enjoyable.

Some of these you may have heard of, and others are just common sense. But if there's one thing I have learned: Common sense ain't that common!

Tip and Trick Number One

When I first started to learn about trading "systems" I read about a short-term system to enter into strong trends. The goal was to ensure that a trader enter only in established trends and therefore increase the chances of follow-through. It worked miserably! On chart after chart, the entries would only lead to a reversal almost three out of four times. Most of the signals led to false breakouts so much so that it became a running joke that since it failed so much, we should do the opposite.

Fast-forward a decade. As I began teaching more students, there would be one situation that would inevitably occur: missed entries. Trading Forex is a 24 hour pursuit and we're just not always going to be home or at the computer or even awake when a trade occurs. This little technique is no guarantee but it gives us another shot at an entry if the initial one was missed. There is one important guideline though: The initial profit target cannot have been reached already... that would nullify an "entry." Here's a great tip when considering your profit targets: If the first target is only 10 to 12 pips away, I will often use the second profit target because the first is too close, so keep that in mind.

Ok, now that we know when we can use this, let's learn how... the technique is simple averaging. If you miss your buy on a long, average the last four lows, use that as your new entry price. If a sell is missed, average the last four highs. Let me say this: You will not always get your fill, and that's the point. This is a "second-chance" entry and if it doesn't meet our price, we move on. This can also be a way to enter on swing trades since this meets the swing trading criteria of buying pullbacks in an uptrend or shorting bounces in a downtrend.

Tip and Trick Number Two:

The banks will often "clear" the market out. Remember psychological numbers? Well, anytime you are in the market with the rest of the crowd you are susceptible to a little game the banks play. If you are a commodity futures trader you may already be familiar with this game as the pit traders do it. Because banks (like to trade in the pit) can see orders, they can also see orders stacking at certain levels. Obviously, since they make their money when they execute trades, who can

blame them for taking advantage of this? The public will often place their orders at round numbers. This is another reason we don't want to place our orders at these "common" places and why we keep eye out for psychological price levels (e.g. 1.2200, 0.7100, or 110.50). We want to get in before or after the crowd, not with them. You may have heard people refer to this as "running stops" and all this means is that banks (specifically trading desks) will see a pile of orders sitting at the same level and execute them. Ever hear of "shooting ducks in a barrel?" Well that's exactly what's happening when you place your trades (entries or exits) at psychological our round numbers that will leave you in with the crowd.

Tip and Trick Number Three:

This isn't any secret but I am amazed by how many traders I run across who do not use this strategy to their full advantage. I am talking about contingent orders. As soon as I enter a trade, I will immediately put in two specific orders. One is a stop-loss and the other is a limit order for my profit target. The contingent orders I am referring to are OCO (one cancel other) orders. This allows you to put in two orders, and if one is executed the other will cancel. For example, if your stop-loss is hit, the profit target order will automatically cancel so that you don't have an open order waiting in the market. If I am stepping away from my computer, I will be sure that I update my OCO order with any changes to the stop-loss (i.e., if I need to trail it) and updates the profit target to the next level, if it applies. If I take a trade overnight, then I will go through this process again, making sure that both orders represent any updates I may need to make to the stop and to the profit target. I never want to keep mental stops or profit targets when I am trading. When we plan a trade—that is before we enter the market—we are sane. Once we enter the market...all sanity leaves with a click of the mouse. Listen to me now...believe me later. For this very reason we must preplan our levels so that we don't get carried away with the moment. When we place the contingent order after our entry, we will take the important step of making sure that our carefully made plan is followed.

CHAPTER 25

News "Discounting"

News "Discounting"

We have focused on price action and charting thus far, and while I am a chartist (that means I believe that the news is built into the price action), I do acknowledge that reports can and do affect the markets.

Each currency will typically act in sympathy with the underlying equities market of that country. Here are some relationships to consider: the NYSE and the U.S. dollar, the London FTSE and the pound, the FTSE Eurotop 300 (secondarily the Paris CAC-40 and Frankfurt Xetra Dax) and the euro. In Japan, it's the Nikkei and the yen; in Southeast Asia, it's the Hang Seng; and for the Australian dollar, we look to the ASX All Ordinaries.

Let's review the reports and events to keep an eye out for:

- European Central Bank and U.S. Federal Reserve decisions on interest rates, and Federal Reserve Chairman's semiannual testimony to Congress before the House Financial Services Committee
- Gross Domestic Product (GDP)—Preliminary

- ISM (Index of Supply Managers) and PMI (Purchasing Managers Index)
- Huge news events like elections and war
- Michigan Sentiment Report
- Non-far payroll

Navigating through the price action created by fundamentals is tricky territory. Prices are affected by fundamentals before and after their release. Of course, I am only referring to scheduled reports and releases, which are the most common. So let's talk about why it's said, "Buy the rumor, sell the news."

The "rumor" is merely the consensus before a report or some sort of scheduled news event, like an FOMC rate decision. Since we know some sort of decision is coming, traders will "discount" or make educated guesses as to the result before it is released and position themselves in the market according to the way they think the market will react to the actual news release or decision. So this entire process of discounting is a battle between the consensus and the actual. The reason playing news in this manner is risky—as compared to using the charts—is because a single trader doesn't know what all the other traders of the world have discounted. There are popular sites that list consensus numbers, but these can vary from source to source. We need to know what news was discounted, how much, and when. This is no easy task. *Playing fundamentals in this manner leaves too much to chance, and it does not even begin to address our only objective, which is to find the price at which we should enter and exit.* The question boils down to: Can news help with timing *and* trade management? While news may afford a trader some degree of timing, as we typically know when a scheduled report is being released, it does not offer the price levels that make up trade management. Trade management means that I know:

- At exactly which price a trade becomes valid and I will enter the trade.
- At exactly which price a trade becomes invalid and I will use a stop-loss to exit the trade.

- At exactly which price I will expect the trade to progress to so I can place my profit targets.

News and fundamentals simply cannot give me these precise levels and therefore cannot help me in building my trade. So we can focus on the timing aspect. When news is released, do we want to enter a market at that exact moment? NO. This is high risk as the market is erratic. The true direction is not always shown at this time, either. In fact, many times what you will see is a sharp move in one direction and then a gradual return to the trend that was established before the news release. I refer to the times just before and just after news or a report is released as the "hot zone."

Let's break down how discounting, or the consensus, affects the market. A few rules of thumb will allow you to measure the reaction to a certain degree, not for trade purposes, but simply to understand price action during this time. Remember that reports are not compared from month to month or even from where it was last year at the same time. All that we need to be concerned with is what the actual number is compared to the consensus. It's basic psychology, really: If a report comes in as bad as we expected, then there will not be a huge sell-off because we knew it was coming and discounted it. Occasionally the market will even have a small move upward. With this same sort of reaction in mind, if a report comes in as good as we expected, then there will not be any sizeable rally because we already figured it in. In fact, there will be profit taking in this scenario and prices will slightly sell off.

Chart 25.1

Here's an example of just how reports can play out in a live market. The following is an example of how the U.S. dollar reacted to the May 28 Michigan Sentiment Report. The arrow shows when the report was released (Ch 25.1).

It's only when the actual is much better or worse than the consensus that traders are surprised and will act. An actual much better than consensus will create a rally just as an actual much weaker than the consensus will create a sharp sell-off. It's all about figuring out what was discounted into the market—*and that's a gamble*. While this is helpful when trying to understand market psychology, there is no methodology a trader can use to project price action as it relates to fundamentals, and thus it is not nearly enough to build a trade.

CHAPTER 26

Charting the U.S. Dollar with Other Currencies

Charting the U.S. Dollar with Other Currencies

W hen trading Forex, we don't "directly" trade the U.S. dollar (USD), even though we have six U.S. dollar pairs that allow us to do so indirectly. These pairs are known as the "majors." The majors account for about 90% of daily trading activity.

The strength or weakness of the U.S. dollar can be charted with the U.S. dollar Index (symbol $DXC). Let's take a look at the $DXC (Ch 26.1).

Starting with this view of an intraday 180-minute chart, we see that the USD is currently trading just below the current downtrend line. Note that prices also bounced off the 0.500 Fibonacci level.

So now let's look at the corres ponding EUR/USD chart at that same point on the chart (Ch 26.2). The market is almost inverse of what we see on the $DXC. It isn't a stretch to say that if the $DXC breaks above the downtrend line that the EUR/USD chart will breakdown below the uptrend line.

What we're talking about here is another type of confirmation. I especially find this relationship powerful when looking at the EUR/USD. *Will all markets have such an exact correlation?* No. However, it is powerful to see where the U.S. dollar is trading in relation to the other currency in the pair. It is just as important to see and measure the trendlines, support, and resistance of the USD so that you can see whether it is strong or weak versus the other currencies.

SYMBOL	If this chart is in an uptrend the dollar is . . .
EUR/USD	weaker
GBP/USD	weaker
AUD/USD	weaker
USD/CHF	stronger
USD/CAD	stronger
USD/JPY	stronger

You'll see that when the U.S. dollar is the base currency, it is strong when the underlying chart is in an uptrend (i.e., USD/CHF, USD/CAD, USD/JPY). Now that we have a general understanding of the relationship between these currencies and the U.S. dollar, it is only natural that the next step is to analyze the levels. Now, please don't assume that we are merely matching uptrends with downtrends or support with resistance, it's not that simplistic. There can be correlations between the trend in one market as compared to the U.S. dollar. With that in mind, let's take a look at the following intraday chart of the British pound (Ch 26.3). This is the same interval and time frame as the U.S. dollar chart on Ch 26.2.

There are two near-term support levels (up arrows) and two near-term resistance levels (down arrows). After

Chart 26.1

looking at the U.S. dollar chart and the British pound chart, the most immediate correlation can be found with the downtrend line of the USD and the 0.886 Fibonacci level or support of the GBP.

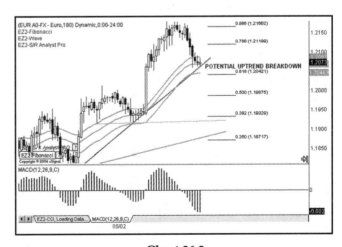

Chart 26.2

For both the EUR and GBP we can see that the $DXC chart could be confirmation, considering that when the EUR and GBP are in uptrends that the U.S. dollar is typically weaker. In both these two pairs, the U.S. dollar is the second currency. Let's examine the market where the U.S. dollar is the base currency.

When looking at the chart of the Swiss franc (Cht 26.4) we see that there is not a near-term support or resistance level to correlate with the $DXC chart (Ch 26.2). The Swiss is in "neutral" territory *(no pun intended!)* as it is trading between the 0.786 Fibonacci level (support) and the 0.618 (resistance). Prices were also consolidating between an uptrend and downtrend, slowly forming a triangle. From this view we see that there is no confirmation here— and no trade—regardless of what the U.S. dollar is doing. *And sometimes knowing when not to trade*

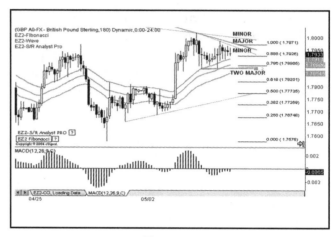

Chart 26.3

can make all the difference. Let's take a look at another market where the U.S. dollar is the base currency.

The circled area shows where USD/JPY has one major and two minor

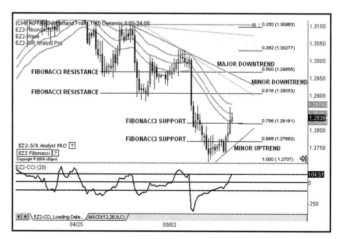

Chart 26.4

downtrend lines to contend with. This chart *does* have correlation with the $DXC chart. While the JPY has pierced all three downtrends, it has yet to close above it. Since we know that if the USD/JPY chart is in an uptrend, the dollar is strong, and this could potentially be excellent confirmation. All entries and exits are about timing. Price action, price patterns, and confirmation are the keys to answering the questions of when and why to enter and exit the market. By analyzing the U.S. dollar we can confirm breakouts and breakdowns in other markets depending on whether they move with or against the U.S. dollar, and this offers us a useful form of confirmation.

More than anything, I want you to really get a feel for what trading in

Chart 26.5

"pairs" means and the relationship with the U.S. dollar. I want to be sure to have the pulse of the U.S. dollar when I am trading—whether I choose to use this sort of secondary confirmation or not. A pair does not move independently of the two currencies that it is composed of. I encourage you to take some time and look at the U.S. dollar chart as you are learning the mannerisms of the major pairs.

CHAPTER 27

Raghee's Rules for Successful Trading

Raghee's Rules for Successful Trading

There no escaping that the way you or I live our lives reflects in our trading. If we are aggressive by nature, so will our trading be. If we are more cautious or tentative in life, we will carry that into our trade.

Recognizing who you are is as simple as placing your first trade because you'll see it up close to the minute the trade either goes in your favor or moves against you.

There are a few rules that have helped me become, and more importantly, stay a trader. Trading is my career. It's not simply a good year or two but rather the culmination of all my years managing the risk of being in the market. It's not just the Forex market that makes me a trader, either. I trade all markets: stocks, futures, and Forex. If it has a chart and liquidity, I will trade it, if I like what I see. Diversification to me means that I do not limit myself to one market or even one style.

Let the charts dictate your stop-losses and profit targets. You now have learned how to begin using trendlines, support, resistance, Fibonacci levels, the Wave, "psychological" numbers, etc., to determine where your entries and exits should be. If the risk-to-reward ratio is not appropriate for your account, neither is that trade setup. (Deciding upon the risk to reward ratio requires that you know at what price level your entry, stop-loss, and initial profit target will be placed. The distance between your entry and stop-loss is considered your "risk," while the distance between your entry and initial profit target is your "reward.") The market doesn't care if you are using a percentage or fixed point stop-loss—these have no bearing on where the market is most likely to move to next, as support and resistance levels do. If once you have set up your trade, you see that the nearest chart-based stop-loss is too far away for your account to absorb, move onto another chart and the next trade. Just remember you must know your stop-loss level and profit targets before you enter the trade.

Recognize, React, Repeat. This is what you want to do each day as a trader.

Much of your time will, and should, be spent recognizing the setups. By doing this, you are also training your eyes to see the difference between good, better, and best trades. The first decision is whether you have a momentum, swing, or no setup. *The last one is the most significant distinction!* Once you recognize what you see on the charts as one of the setups, the next step is to react. Reacting means deciding upon the entry and exit levels that correspond with the setup and as we know for momentum trades, we look for breakouts and breakdowns. For swing trades we are looking to buy pullback in an uptrend and short bounces in a downtrend. Finally, we seek to repeat this process as consistently as possible.

Exit at each predetermined profit target. We want to exit when we can, not when we have to. I will place my order—entry or exit—as the market nears my predetermined level or anytime I have to step away from the computer. There is no hard and fast rule for entries. I will sometimes leave a standing limit order, and other times I will enter as I see my price. For stop-losses and profit targets, I will always leave standing orders, always! Regarding profit targets: If a typical trade for your account size is two lots then by the second profit target, you will be flat. One way I decide how many lots I will enter with is to see how many

profit targets total I can see on the chart. Sometimes there are five and six targets, other times there are only two or three. Of course, this falls second to what is right for your account size. And that leads me to the next rule.

Margin accelerates your winners and losers. There's a saying in motorcycling: "Any Gomer can twist a throttle." Anyone can push the limit, but it's few and far between that you find someone that can bring it back. If you continually trade beyond your capabilities and risk capital, you will lose. When you trade ForeX you are typically trading 50:1 or 100:1, and I've even seen 200:1. While you can make huge profits, always consider that if the market went against you, you would lose at the same rate. Margin makes everything move faster and the more margin, the faster is goes. I've seen new riders on motorcycles that had no business being on a bike with that much horsepower. The lucky ones had a few scares and learned from it. The unlucky ones pushed the limit and never could bring it back.

So what's the answer? We know that trading, like motorcycling, can be a high-risk activity. Just as a new rider should learn the art of riding a motorcycle on a smaller bike with less horsepower, so should a trader begin with a mini account. I love the idea of mini accounts.

Almost all brokerages offer these types of accounts. Here's how they work.

You can trade all the majors in a mini account. The lot size in a mini is 1/10 the size of a full size lot, and the pip value is $1 versus $10. Once you have learned a methodology, back-tested it, and acquainted yourself with an execution platform, your next step is learning what it's like to trade with real money. With a mini account you can benefit from real market action, the nerves, fear and greed that accompany it, and still not lose your shirt. At $1 a pip you can make plenty of mistakes (and you will!) without falling into a financial abyss.

Forget papertrading. It is absolutely worthless as a trading substitute. If you wanted to acquaint yourself with an execution platform and practice order execution, fantastic! Go ahead and papertrade. If you wanted to test a new trading idea, great! Go ahead, back-test and papertrade the idea. If you want to see how you can trade with an established methodology, use a mini account. You will never be able to recreate the feeling of being in a real money trade with papertrading. When you trade with real money, even in a mini account, you will still feel the burst of adrenaline when you enter a trade, the exhilaration when you are making money, and the pit in your stomach when you are losing.

These are all kinesthetic reactions to a visceral activity. When our money is on the line, we are emotionally invested, and we pay better and sharper attention to what we are doing than if the trade was taking place in the "land of make-believe." Even now, I always keep a mini account open because if I find myself on a losing streak (or I want to experiment with a new trading idea), rather than retreating from the market completely, I will review my errors and make my comeback...using my mini account.

Draw trendlines, support and resistance rather then looking for specific patterns. If you are looking for a specific pattern, you will find it on the charts. It's like looking at the clouds and seeing a bunny...we see it because we want to. Find all the lines and levels on a chart, and if a pattern is there, you will see it.

Find the trend before you enter any trade. The scanning step of each trade setup is when we check for trend direction on each of our time frames. The prep work step is vital for this very reason. Finding the trend is directly related to the type of trade you will set up. The Wave is the best way I have found to make sure I am in the ideal environment for a momentum or swing trade. When I am swing trading, I want to see the Wave traveling at noon to two o'clock for buying opportunities and the Wave traveling at four to six o'clock for shorting opportunities. When I am momentum trading, the most ideal Wave direction is sideways or three o'clock. There will be occasions that you will see your trendlines, support, and resistance forming momentum trading patterns like triangles and rectangles, yet you may have an up or down trending Wave. In these situations you are getting mixed signals, and your best course of action is to look at another time frame to see if the signals line up more clearly with *either* a swing or momentum trade.

Use your "ands" your "ors" to plan your trade. Any trade is a process of asking and answering questions. We want everything to be right when we enter a trade. It reminds me of what my husband taught me about fishing. I love to go fishing...if I got the Internet on our boat, I'd probably never come back to shore. Sure you can go out and try to catch fish, but you won't necessarily catch anything just because you dropped your line in the water. It's best to know what you're fishing for *and* have the right bait *and* be out at the time of day the fish feed *and* in the right water temperature *and* fish with the tide. Basically you want to put as much as you can in your favor so you're in the right place at the right time. Great fishermen do this, so do great traders. They line up all the

"ands." If one or more of the things we look for change, it can affect our plan and results. For example, we would not go fishing (or we would be less likely to catch fish) if the water temperature is too low *or* the tide is wrong *or* the bait is wrong *or* the barometer is dropping.

Don't chase a trade. When we trade a 24 hour market we will find ourselves missing entries. It's inevitable because we must sleep, go out, eat dinner, etc. While we don't chase a market, we will use our charts to find the next best way to enter the trade. Those levels could be based upon Fibonacci levels, the four-day method, the Wave, or even psychological price levels. If we don't get our fill at the specified price, we move on. However, since we have learned to set up both momentum and swing trades, we can use both to help us out. For example, if we missed a momentum entry, and a trend develops from the initial breakout or breakdown, we can look to see if we can get a swing set up.

Be thankful. We live in a time when we have instant access to the markets, quotes, and charts. We have governing bodies that regulate the markets and brokerages. We live in a time when all the tools that allow us to be traders are accessible from our homes. Be thankful for all the opportunities on the charts and in your life.

CHAPTER 28

A Day in the Life of a ForeX Trader

A Day in the Life of a ForeX Trader

What's an educational book without some real-world application? That's what we're going to do right now! This is a "look over my shoulder" view of how I approach a typical day of trading.

Not that there is a "typical" day! In fact, a trading day begins the night before and ends the morning after. For example, if I am preparing for Tuesday, the work actually begins Monday evening and will effect Wednesday's setups. I have to confess, I usually don't like trading Mondays. I will typically keep the pulse of the market on Monday...and that means the *whole* market. Because I trade stocks, futures, and Forex, I will scan the daily charts of the individual stocks (including mutual funds) and futures contracts on Monday. This does not take all day but it is a great day for me to look outside the Forex market and do analyze my charts, all while keeping an eye on any developments in the Forex. On Friday I will typically do something similar. I will evaluate my trades, look at the week's action and plan my exits of open intraday trades. And that brings up a great point about my intraday trades:

Unless I have a large cushion and a small position remaining, I will typically exit my trades some time on Friday. I am not a fan of taking positions over the weekend. This is not a hard and fast rule! It's just my preference...I just wanted to make that clear.

I want you to make your own decisions concerning how you manage your trading life! These are the realities and decisions you make when you adapt a 24-hour market. I don't want Forex to become your whole life. A lot of traders teeter on the precarious brink of letting the markets take over their lives because it's open all day and night. I've been there, so I have to tell you this: Trading is as much about making a living as it is having a life. The freedom of time, the freedom to work from home, the freedom to set your own schedule, the freedom of being your own boss...these are all reasons that people also consider trading. It doesn't have to be a full-time pursuit and that's one of the unique features of the Forex—it will fit into anyone's schedule!

My most active days are Tuesdays, Wednesdays, and Thursdays for the very reasons I mentioned before. So let's examine how a trading day develops. First thing I'll do Monday evening—in preparation for Tuesday—

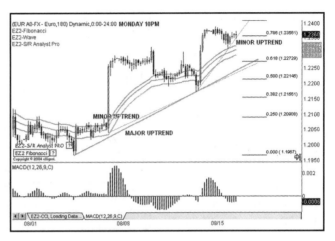

Chart 28.1

is look to see if there are any setups that are close to confirming. Since 30- and 60-minute set ups are more likely to confirm while I am asleep, I will focus on the 180, 240, and daily charts the evening before. Here is the view of the euro on the 180, 240, and daily charts (Charts 28.1, 28.2, 28.3).

First thing to notice is that I have marked the uptrend and downtrends, supports, and resistance level. Be sure to note any Fibonacci retracements and extensions that will act as near-term support and resistance levels. As you can see, some charts

show a more imminent setup. For example, the 180-minute chart has a minor uptrend that prices are currently resting on and the daily chart shows an asymmetrical or pennant setup. Both of these

Chart 28.2

are momentum set ups and I know at what price level they may break out or break down by the charts. This makes it easier to plan ahead because I know where the trade will become valid, which is my entry price. I also can decide upon my stop-loss and profit targets. Here's a view of the 180-minute euro with entry, stop-loss, and profit target analysis (Ch 28.4).

Since these are not setups that I am likely to take until the next morning, there are some things that I would like to see before I pull the trigger. First, I would rather see the Wave on this chart level out or flatten into a more three o'clock direction if I am going to take the breakdown trade. If this doesn't happen, a pullback into the Wave could create a bounce, and then I am not likely to see the 0.618 profit target. These are the kind of considerations that you take into account on the evening

Chart 28.3

before. Let's follow along with the 180-minute chart and take a look at the view on Tuesday morning (Chart 28.5). I see that I have missed the minor uptrend breakdown...and I also know that the

Chart 28.4

Wave could create a bounce. I have to balance both the charting levels in my mind to make a decision.

The view at 6 AM shows that minor uptrend line broke and that the Wave seems to have caught the fall as we see the wick (low) bottomed out near the middle line of the Wave. These are scenarios we discussed. I have a saying that I follow when I trade. I want to consider all the possibilities as they relate to my tools. *I don't mind being wrong—that's part of trading—but I don't want to be surprised.* This is a great time to mention economic reports. It is helpful to have a morning checklist. Let's briefly discuss that now:

Each morning I evaluate what happened while I was sleeping. Frankly I don't always get up that early…but typically no later than seven o'clock. After I see what the charts look like I will head over to a site like *briefing.com* to see what (if any) reports are scheduled to be released. Since we are already familiar with the reports that we know affect the Forex markets, we will be on the lookout for those specific reports and events.

Chart 28.5

Up until now I have focused on the euro. Let's shift gears and take a look at some other markets and how they are trading Tuesday morning. On each one of these charts I have marked the levels that I am watching. These levels define that current market environment and also allow me to see if I will be setting up a potential momentum or swing trade.

On the chart of the British pound (Ch 28.6) we see that the market is currently trading at the 0.382 Fibonacci level, which is support. The Wave has been traveling in a chop (no established direction) since August 1. The market does not have a near-term setup; however I do know the current price action points to a momentum setup rather than a swing setup. The lack of (1) an established trend, (2) the bracketing of the market by the horizontal resistance, and (3) support of the major trend make this distinction clear.

The Aussie (Ch 28.7) has some chart levels that prices are currently sandwiched between. The 0.618 and 0.500 Fibonacci retracement levels are acting as support and resistance. There are also few uptrends line we see. The first is a rather steep, minor uptrend line. While prices have broken that level, the Fibonacci levels are more likely to be better confirmation. The two trendlines, far below current price action, will most likely not be in play as any kind of entry trigger, but we will keep an eye on them if we have a short entry because they will be support levels and therefore possible profit targets.

The Swiss franc (Ch 28.8), or "swissy," is trading in an established downtrend and the Wave confirms this fact. Sim-

Chart 28.6

ilar to the Aussie chart, a Fibonacci level is currently acting as resistance, and there is a horizontal support level with two touchpoints keeping prices up. Remember that support represents buy-

Chart 28.7

ing. Together these two levels are bracketing the market. This chart is a contradiction in some ways because we see traits of both types of setups that we trade. The bracketing is momentum based, while the established downtrend and four to six o'clock Wave point to a swing setup. The decision to take a momentum breakout trade would be contratrend. However a breakdown trade would be trading with the established trend...and I would much rather be trading with the established trend. Remember, ideally we want to see a sideways Wave when we set up breakout/breakdown trades. We could also consider the current candle, which is touching the middle line of the Wave. This could easily be a bounce that could be shorted within the context of the downtrend. What is most important to consider is that because we are using the same tools with a set of guidelines, we can choose to take the trade that suits us best and that works best with the current trend. If the Wave levels out, we can talk about an upside momentum breakout. These are excellent examples of the deci-

Chart 28.8

sions we must make every day. And if you noticed it is very much a process of elimination.

The chart of the Canadian dollar (Ch 28.9) also has a downtrend as defined by the four to six o'clock direction of the Wave. The 1.272 Fibonacci extension is currently resistance. Just above that we have the Wave sloping down and this will be resistance as well. This only near-term setup in this chart would be a short into either the Fibonacci extension (aggressive) or a short into a potential pullback into the levels of the Wave.

What we have just done on these four charts is put all the tools and ideas together to analyze the current market. One benefit of Forex trading is the longer time frames we track. Since we are only getting new candles, every 30, 60, 180, or 240 minutes on our intraday charts we have some time to digest price action and ask questions. These setups are not rushed nor are they sudden. You'll notice that we preplan our entries, and in that way this approach to trading is not a knee-jerk reaction to prices.

Chart 28.9

Consider that as each market continues to trade, there will be new lines and levels that develop. We must stay on top of changes in price action that either make our old levels irrelevant or create new ones. I will track the six majors on five time frames, as you already know. That can be a lot of updating, and for years I did this manually. It was no small task. I would scan the markets intraday and make sure that I had the most recent major and minor trendlines, the most recent horizontal support and resistance levels, and the most recent and relevant Fibonacci retracements and extensions. I knew that if I wasn't vigilant to this task of updating the charts, I could miss entries and incorrectly gauge my profit

targets and stop-loss levels. Last fall I decided I needed to take advantage of new features on my eSignal platform. I found and helped develop a secret weapon. All the tools on my charts are automated. That means that as soon as I bring up a chart, regardless of the market or time frame, my software will automatically show me all the trendlines, support, resistance, Fibonacci levels, and more—all set to my specifications. Be sure to visit *www.raghee.com* for examples of how the software works.

We have examined the 180- minute charts. I will go through this process with all five time frames. One of the best tools to accomplish this task quickly and effectively is to use the Wave as I described in Chap. 17, "Prep Work."

When the Wave is moving from noon to two o'clock, or from four to six o'clock, we know that we will most likely be setting up a swing trade and if we trade against the direction of the Wave it is a contratrend trade. When the Wave is traveling at three o'clock we know that we will be on the lookout for a momentum trade, typically a triangle or sideways channel. It's an easy rule of thumb you can use as you gain experience trading the setups on the Forex. It will allow you to narrow down the type of levels you are looking for and be able to focus on the specific price action that will affect your entry the most. I recommend that you follow the three steps as you learn to trade the Forex before you break the rules. I encourage you to take this time to learn the rules, in fact, visit *www.raghee.com* for more articles, charts, and video lessons that will reinforce what you have learned in this book.

Our job as traders is to handle the risk of being in the market. And believe me, it is a risk. While we talk about risk/reward ratios, it is the risk element that will affect you the most. Always keep this in mind when you trade. Fear is not a bad feeling, as long it does not paralyze you. Respect the power of the market. Trading reminds me of a quote I heard from race car driver Lyn St. James. (Lyn St. James was the first woman to win the Indy 500.) And even though it is about the risk involved in race car driving, I found it applies to the market as well.

I love going fast. It's such an exhilaration to control the powerful piece of equipment. Of course, it's a risk. But risk is like a muscle: You exercise it, you learn how to control it, you get better at it. You can't get too comfortable with yourself though. You have to keep pushing that muscle to make it grow. Auto racing is genderless; the car doesn't know the difference and no one can even see that it's a woman driving. No one judges me by my smile or personality, but by my results. What I've learned is that you have to learn the rules, play by the rules, win by the rules, and then you can change the rules.

CHAPTER ㉙

Conversation with Raghee Horner

Conversation with Raghee Horner by Linus K. Ahnis

I*t's a Friday morning and I am nervously preparing for an interview with Raghee. She's told me how important this section is to her, and I am hoping that I can ask the questions that the readers would ask if they had the opportunity. Raghee chose to conduct the interview at her home office. She has an office out east on the intercoastal and I was hoping we would conduct the interview there, as the view is great.*

But she's mentioned that she's watching the local fishing report, and I figure she's being funny. I arrive at her home at 8:30 AM on Tuesday and sure enough she has the local fishing report show on the one of the two televisions she has in her home office. Funny, I thought traders are glued to CNBC. Raghee is glancing at about eight charts spread over two flat screens; she tells me they are the six "majors," the U.S. dollar Cash Index, and the S&P E-Mini. I ask her about the E-Mini and she replies "I'll trade it if I see one of my three setups. I'll watch it 'til about 11:30." I remember that Raghee tells me that she watches stocks, futures, and Forex and encourages her students

to do the same. She offers me a cup of coffee and seems ready to start our conversation.

Thanks for taking some time this morning for a few questions. I see you've got your eye on the two monitors in front of you. Two screens seem unusual when I have seen traders in front of 8 and 10 monitors. And where's the CNBC?

Thank *you* for taking the time to come over. As for the monitors, I don't like sitting in front of more than two. Frankly, with my style I have often traded from my laptop. Most of my scanning is done last thing in the evening and first thing in the morning, so I don't have to watch too many charts intraday because I have typically narrowed down the time frames that I will trade on each market. You can see here that I have eight charts total, and six of them are for the Forex. I am not a "rapid fire" trader. And with a 24-hour market I don't feel the need to press for trades since I will usually see another setup coming around the corner on one of my five time frames. I watch CNBC in the morning as the reporting from CNBC Asia and CNBC Europe is helpful. After that I will keep one television on CNBC and another on ESPN. This fishing report is on each week, and I like to catch it before the weekend. Surprised?

I admit I am a little surprised. So you trade watch five time frames?

Actually I *scan* five time frames for each of the six currency pairs that I track. I look for which has the cleanest setup and which may be the closest to an actual entry. I'll then focus on that one chart for that currency pair. So in that regard I am not using multiple time frame confirmation.

I see. Could you explain what you mean by "multiple time frame confirmation"?

Sure. Early on when I began trading I would always hear the words "multiple time frame confirmation" and that it is something we should look for. Frankly, it made sense when someone explained it but it just didn't ring true when I began trading. "Multiple time frame confirmation" is basically when you look at two (or more) charts of the same market but on two different time frames. One could be the daily and the other could be the 60-minute. If you were looking to trade on the 60-minute you would want to "confirm" that the daily chart was also trending in the same direction. In other words, you would want to enter long on the 60 minute only when the daily is an uptrend. That's a simplified example. Regardless, I didn't feel that a trade on the 60-minute chart had anything to do with the trend on the daily. To me, one is a short-term trade and the other is a longer-term trade because I am getting a new candle every 60 minutes on one chart versus one candle each day.

I began to question why I should confirm one time frame with another and decided that with my approach I could confirm the trend or lack of trend with the Wave and then decide upon entries and exits with trendlines, support and resistance, and Fibonacci levels. I treat each time frame on its own merit and do not look to other time frames to confirm direction.

Other time frames may have better, cleaner setups, a better risk/reward ratio, etc., so I am simply looking for the setup that looks best to me.

Let me ask you...why do you like teaching? I mean writing a book is no small task. I imagine that it takes time from your trading.

There are times I ask myself that same question. Seriously, though, I love teaching. It's personally very rewarding to positively affect a person's life. I have been lucky because, as I have said over and over again: I have some great students. They are wonderful people that I consider my friends.

There is so much I have wanted to share for so long that it seems that the book wrote itself. It really didn't take much time at all. After all I was simply sharing how and what I have been doing for over a decade. I don't mean to impress anyone with that, but it's just easier to write about things you know and things you do every day. I did it because I couldn't find a decent book to recommend to my students that wanted to Forex trade. And definitely, it does take from my trading. On the other hand, it is a tremendous honor. I never thought that I would be asked to write a book at 32. It's a dream come true to be able to have an international platform from which I can reach so many people. I'm thankful.

Teaching holds me a to a higher standard. I have to walk the talk. My students keep me honest and they keep me looking for better ways to share ideas. In many ways, teaching forced me to develop and stick with my step-by-step methodology. Sometime I really get sick of hearing how much of an "art" trading is. That's not to say it's not an art or a craft, it is! But just as you can learn how to paint or how to sculpt, you can learn how to trade. There are people who will paint and sculpt better than others but that doesn't mean that an individual can't create their own art.

In fact, one of my near term "teaching" goals is to see that trading/chart analysis become a college course.

How do you begin a typical day?

I try to wake up early enough where I can catch some of London's morning trading. That's not always a reality, though. I'm in South Florida, so that means London is five hours ahead. I want to be ready, at the latest, by 7:30 AM EST. I'm not one to tell you that you have to be up at 3 am. If you can or if you are already up, you can trade the London open and the U.S. open. It's a great "market overlap" as I explained in the book. If New York is the center of the stock universe, then London is the center of the Forex universe. After I take a quick look at any of my trades that I held overnight, I try to squeeze in a quick workout and a cup of coffee before I sit down at the computer. A quick workout is better than the coffee for waking up. After my workout, I will scan the five time frames for each of the "majors."

Could you tell me what the "majors" are?

OK. Quickly, those are the U.S. dollar pairs. The euro/U.S. dollar, the pound/U.S. dollar, the Aussie/U.S. dollar, the U.S. dollar/Swiss, the U.S. dollar/Canada, and the U.S. dollar/yen.

So I'm scanning through these pairs on the five time frames: the 30-, 60-, 180-, 240-minute and the daily chart. I'm looking to see which are in trends versus sideways markets. The Wave accomplishes this for me, quickly and easily as I explained in Chap. 17, "Prep Work."

I will also be sure I know what relevant economic reports or events are going to take place because these create those volatile "hot zones." I do not trade based upon reports. But many times the reports will be the trigger that creates the breakout or breakdown, pullback, or bounce that my chart setup was waiting for.

That reminds me of something you wrote in the book: "Chartists believe that the news is built into price action."

Absolutely! I live by that. I never let the emotion and excitement of news effect my chart set up. Price gets me in and price gets me out. News can't do this. News can't tell me at what price to enter and exit. On its own, news can't be the reason for me to enter a trade. This is because of discounting. Discounting is the action behind the saying "buy the rumor, sell the news."

On a personal note, I've heard that your mother is a trader?

Yeah, well, it's actually a testament to my Ma's tenacity. She wasn't a trader really, but she did market time mutual funds, unknowingly and successfully! My father passed away when I was 15 and it was just my Ma, my sister, and I. We were like the Three Musketeers. She knew that she had to make the most of what money she had to raise two kids. She started reading about the markets and mutual funds, and even though she didn't know it she was studying price action and seasonal events to time her purchases. Over time she noticed that it was working and she built a small amount of money into enough to plan her retirement, open a business, and help put two kids through college.

I've heard that you have automated your charting tools? Is this true?

Yes, but I did not automate them myself. In fact, I have a brilliant programmer who did the coding and I lent my trading knowledge for some of the particulars. The tools are actually his and I pay for them like anyone else. And I am happy to do so too! The tools are the best I have ever used when it comes to automating trendlines, support, resistance, Fibonacci, candlestick patterns, and more. I literally can turn each tool on or off as I follow my three-step setup. I use eSignal as my charting provider. I have done so for many, many years and the tools work on eSignal. In fact, when I develop a new charting tool or approach I like to automate it.

Why did you want to do that? You don't seem to be a fan of systems.

It's not a system. I can't be more clear than that. They are automated tools. They don't replace your brain, they are simply tools of that I have found save me time, and if used correctly, increase my accuracy. I also found that it shortens the learning curve for my students. Another point is that if I can automate a tool that means there is a method that anyone can follow because there are steps that a trader could duplicate. For example, when I use automated trendlines the program knows to connect certain highs and lows in order to draw the line. A trader could do the same thing but the program will do it more consistently and much quicker. However, I would never recommend automating any tool that you cannot first manually do yourself. If you don't know how to manually draw a trendline, you should not automate it and start trading. But I really can't hide my enthusiasm for the tools. When I first started using them, I used to put my manually analyzed chart up next to the automated ones. Not only did the automated ones find the same levels I did, they found others that my eye could not see. Even better the program updates the levels as price action changes so I am never looking at dated lines and levels, Fibonacci levels, minor highs, and minor lows, etc. They really have had an impact on my trading unlike any other tool I have ever used. I only wish I could take credit for having developed them!

I know that you use the Wave, trendlines, support, resistance, and Fibonacci. How did you decide upon these tools and not others? Do you ever use any other tools? Like I know you mentioned you use the CCI as a confirmation tool on one of your setups.

I naturally gravitated toward these tools because they were the first that I learned. I think most traders learn about trendlines, support, and resistance very early on in their studies. Maybe not Fibonacci right away though. The bottom line was that these tools addressed the questions that I felt needed to be answered before every trade: where I should enter, where my stop-loss should be, and where my profit targets are. Since these tools worked well I didn't concern myself with other tools. *I think that's a quality successful traders have: They know when to stick with what works*. I also noticed that I did not care to have indicators dictate where and when I should trade. I did realize that they made for excellent confirmation tools. So that's one of the reasons I use the CCI with the Wave in the combo setup I outline in the book. Another indicator I like to use this the MACD histo-

gram. In fact, I mention in the book how I first used the MACD as a confirmation tool in my E-Mini trading and how I now use it to confirm momentum trades.

I see that you have been taking some screen captures of your charts. Do you study these?

That's a great question. I used to do that a lot. I used a screen capture tool called Snag It and would take snapshots of setups that I had analyzed I would study all these snapshots and soon there started to be similar patterns that followed through and tendencies that I noticed. So early on it was a helpful tool. eSignal has actually incorporated a capture tool into the platform, which is great. They also have a playback feature that allows you to fast-forward and rewind charts like a VCR so that you can see what a chart has done in the past. You can test ideas. And my automated software will also work in this mode so you can test ideas by rewinding to a past date and play one candle at a time or jump forward to see how it played out.

Right now though I am capturing these images for an upcoming project. I read a book many years ago that followed a trader over the course of a month. He discussed all his trades, why he took them, when and why he took profits or got stopped out. He even went into the details of what happens when his alarm clock doesn't go off and when "life" interferes with the trading process. We don't trade in a bubble. In fact, just last week I was dealing with an impending hurricane and how that could affect my family, my home, my phone and electricity, my boat, etc. These are real concerns that have nothing to do with trading yet still affect my trading. This particular book inspired me more than any other I had read to write a book myself. I thought this personal aspect of the book was excellent. I knew that one day I would do the same in the Forex market, and that's what I am doing. I will be discussing all my trades over the course of a month so that other traders can "look over my shoulder" and see exactly what I am doing. They can see the reality of a trader's day. They will also be able to see how the "three steps" come to life. I think more than anything though they will see that I do exactly what I teach in this book. In the end, they will be able to see how the month worked out for me: wins and losses. I've seen too many teachers that like to focus on wins because, let's face it, it's always impressive to show people how much you made. But frankly, no one wins all the

time and I felt sharing my losses are an important part of this project. Teachers that don't share their mistakes, and losses are really robbing their students of valuable lessons. I know that I can trade well and I don't need my ego stroked. So why not share with those willing to learn that "pros" make mistakes too, that we're just like anyone else, and that all our trades are not winners.

How many pairs would you recommend a new trader watch when they are just starting out?

Super question. In fact I just got this question when I spoke to a local trading group. My answer is this: Track at least two, never one! And here's why:

When you track just one market you will tend to squeeze trades or force them because you have no other market to track. Let me give you an example. There is a phenomenon I noticed when the E-Mini S&P began gaining widespread popularity. I think one of the catalysts was because the minimum account requirement for daytrading stocks was increased to $25,000. Now all of a sudden a lot of active traders didn't have the money to trade stocks. The E-Mini S&P seemed a great option. So these traders that often had five, ten, twenty, or even a hundred stocks that they tracked everyday, had one futures market. I hope you see where I am heading with this . . . what happened was so interesting to me, and also something that I discovered I was susceptible to myself!

These traders has formerly been able to scan for setups from a number of choices. Now they had one. Many day-traders feel that they must stay busy and that means they think they have to trade. Sometimes the choice to stay flat, to stay out of the market is the "best trade." So all these new futures traders are over-trading the E-Mini because it's the only market they are watching. And in the back of their head they know that if they don't trade, they don't make any money. But it works the other way too! Bad trades take away your money! If these traders had another market to watch, or even better another three or four, they could have picked from the best setup or at least the setup that suited them best. They could have choices for momentum versus swing trades like I talk about in the book. They could even take certain trades based upon a favorable risk/ reward ratio.

I like how you put these seemingly unre-lated events together.

Thanks! Remember that we're not really trading the Forex market or the stock market or the futures market. We are trading other traders and their fear, greed, and emotion. Each candle (or bar) represents opinion and we are simply tracking and monitoring that opinion. If you always keep the human or the psy-chological element in mind you will never be surprised by price action.

Finally, what is your best trading tool?

No question about it. It's confidence. Without confidence in my tools, con-fidence in my strategy/methodology/ whatever you'd like to call it, and with-out confidence in myself I could not be a successful trader. I've seen too many smart people who have little to no confi-dence in their chosen tools and in them-selves. Inevitably they look for other people or other things to make deci-sions for them. For example, they will buy subscriptions to newsletters and chat rooms without really studying and understanding the underlying method-ology. Or they will buy a system that makes all the decisions for them. Anything to keep them from being the one in control and therefore avoiding being the reason the trade went badly. Nobody wants to blame himself or her-self. We're all guilty of that. With this type of crutch it is never our fault. And when one crutch doesn't work, these traders will move on to the next. It's really a vicious cycle.

So how do we prevent that from happening?

First we have to learn an approach that is tried and true. We should begin with the basics from which everything else is built. For example, before you learn chart patterns you should learn to draw trendlines, support, and resistance, which are the building blocks of most chart patterns as I discuss in the book. We should find tools that will allow us to trade in both a swing and momentum style. We should learn how to read price charts before we even think about laying a single indicator on them. We should understand how to differentiate a trending market from a choppy market by looking at the price chart. I think these are all part of the foundation we must build.

CHAPTER ③⓪

www.raghee.com

www.raghee.com

I saved this for last because I have been in your shoes.

I can't tell you how many times I have finished a great trading book and wanted to see some recent charts and articles the author may have written. Once you have read (and re-read) this book, the ideas and strategies we've discussed will be more clear. I do know—*from experience*—that during the early stage of either learning how to trade or learning a new approach can leave you with questions. That's exactly why *www.raghee.com* is available to you! It's a one-step reference for all things related to this book. Personally, I love the Internet. I just can't get enough of it. I love that it allows me to keep in touch with students, I love that it allows me to meet and correspond with fellow traders, I love that it is an accessibleplace that I can share ideas.

At *www.raghee.com,* I will post charts as well as have articles, lessons, and online videos relating to foundational trading concepts as well as some of the advanced strategies I am working on. It's the perfect way to keep in touch with me. And I'd be honored if you let me know how you are doing with your studies and trading! I will also be offering limited time specials and trials to the products and services I offer. Think of it as an "insider's club." You will also be able to find my online and appearance schedule at the site. I will be conducting online "webinars" that allow you to see my actual charts in real-time video as well as hear me...all over your computer, live!

I have noticed that after a people read any kind of instructional or educational book, two things can happen. One, they put the information to work, practice, and make their goals a reality. Second, and more often, the book finds the shelf or closet, the knowledge slowly becomes a memory, and the people are right back from where they started. I find this happens mainly because there is no help, no guidance, and no one to give the readers a helping hand. From the moment I began writing I knew that I didn't want this to be the end of the dialogue between you, the reader, and myself. It wouldn't be fair to you or to me. I want to help you put this knowledge to work or at least test it and see if it's for you. I invite you to see all the free information I have included at my website. I encourage you to make sure that the knowledge in this book and at *www.raghee.com* helps you reach your goals. Thanks for your time!

Yours in Trading,

Glossary of ForeX Trading Terms

This glossary clarifies some of the technical terms used in this book and is intended to assist you in your goal of becoming a successful Forex trader.

A

AAA　American Arbitration Association

Aftermarket　Trading activity in a security immediately following its offering to the public.

Agency Order　An order that a broker/dealer executes for the account of a customer with another professional or retail investor and for which a commission is typically charged.

All-or-None (AON)　A type of order instructing the exchange or market maker to execute the entire order quantity at the stated price (or better) or none of it.

Appreciation　A currency is said to appreciate when it strengthens in price in response to market demand.

Arbitrage　Arbitrage involves the simultaneous purchase of a security in one market and the sale of it or a derivative product in another market to profit from price differentials between the two markets.

Arbitration　A method where conflict between two or more parties is resolved by impartial persons—arbitrators—who are knowledgeable in the areas in controversy.

Around　Dealer lingo used in quoting when the forward premium/discount is near parity. For example, "two-two around" would translate into 2 points to either side of the present spot.

Ask Rate　The rate at which a financial instrument is offered for sale (as in bid/ask spread).

Asset Allocation　Investment practice that divides funds among different markets to achieve diversification for risk management purposes and/or expected returns consistent with an investor's objectives.

B

Back Office Refers to the clerical operations of a brokerage company that support the trading operations. Their responsibilities include trade settlement, order confirmations, technical support, record keeping, and regulatory compliance.

Balance Sheet An accounting statement reflecting the firm's financial condition in terms of assets, liabilities, and net worth (ownership). In a balance sheet, net worth = assets + liabilities.

Balance of Trade The value of a country's export minus its imports.

Base Currency In general terms, the base currency is the currency in which an investor or issuer maintains its book of accounts. In the FX markets, the U.S. dollar is normally considered the base currency for quotes, meaning that quotes are expressed as a unit of $1 USD per the other currency quoted in the pair. The primary exceptions to this rule are the British pound, the euro, and the Australian dollar.

Bear Market A market distinguished in which prices are low or declining; a bull market is one in which prices are high or rising.

Bid Rate The rate at which a trader is willing to buy currency.

Bid/Ask Spread The difference between the bid and offer price, and the most widely used measure of market liquidity.

Big Figure Dealer expression referring to the first few digits of an exchange rate. These digits rarely change in normal market fluctuations, and therefore are omitted in dealer quotes, especially in times of high market activity. For example, a USD/yen rate might be 107.30/107.35, but would be quoted verbally without the first three digits, e.g., "30/35."

Book In a professional trading environment, a book is the summary of a trader's or desk's total positions.

Breakdown A drop below a level of support that is usually accompanied by a significant rise in volume.

Breakout A rise in a security's price above a resistance level that is usually accompanied by a significant rise in volume.

Broker An individual or firm who acts as an intermediary between a buyer and seller for a fee or commission. In contrast, a dealer commits capital and takes one side of a position, hoping to earn a spread (profit) by closing out the position in a subsequent trade with another party.

Bretton Woods Agreement of 1944 An agreement that established fixed foreign exchange rates for major currencies, provided for central bank intervention in the currency markets, and pegged the price of gold at USD $35 per ounce. The agreement lasted until 1971, when President Nixon overturned the Bretton Woods agreement and established a floating exchange rate for the major currencies.

Bundesbank Germany's Central Bank.

C

Cable Trader lingo referring to the sterling/U.S. dollar exchange rate. So-called because the rate was originally transmitted via a transatlantic cable beginning in the mid-1800s.

Candlestick Chart A chart that indicates the trading range for the day as well as the opening and closing price. If the open price is higher than the close price, the rectangle between the open and close price is shaded if the close price is higher than the open price, that area of the chart is not shaded.

Capital The total amount of money the trader has to trade with. Or, the term that refers to the money that the individual has accumulated and is available to produce more money.

Cash Coins and currency that is readily available.

Central Bank A government or quasi-governmental organization that manages a country's monetary policy. For example, the U.S. central bank is the Federal Reserve, and the German central bank, noted in the glossary, is the Bundesbank.

Chartist An individual who uses charts and graphs and interprets historical data to discover trends and forecast future movements. Also referred to as Technical Trader.

Clearance The conclusion (settlement) of an exchange of securities.

Close The price of the last transaction of a security on a particular trading day.

Collateral Something given to secure a loan or as a guarantee of performance.

Commission Fees paid to a broker for executing a trade based on the number of shares traded or the dollar amount of the trade.

Confirmation Formal memorandum from a broker to a client giving details of a securities transaction.

Contagion The tendency of an economic crisis to spread from one market to another. In 1997, political instability in Indonesia caused high volatility in their domestic currency, the Rupiah. From there, the contagion spread to other Asian emerging currencies, and then to Latin America, and is now referred to as the "Asian Contagion."

Contract The standard unit of trading.

Country Risk Risk associated with a cross-border transaction, including but not limited to legal and political conditions.

Cross Rate The exchange rate between any two currencies that are considered non-standard in the country where the currency pair is quoted. For example, in the United States, a GBP/JPY quote would be considered a rate, whereas in United Kingdom or Japan it would be one of the primary currency pairs traded.

Currency Any form of money issued by a government or central bank and used as legal tender and a basis for trade.

Currency Risk The probability of an adverse change in exchange rates.

Customer (Account) Statement Also called the month-end statement. This document states the customer's positions and activity. It must be sent out quarterly, but if there is monthly activity in the account, it is sent out monthly.

D

Day Trading Refers to positions which are opened and closed on the same trading day. The opposite of the buy and hold strategy.

Dealer Any person or company in the business of buying and selling securities for his/her own account, through a broker or otherwise. Usually, they will also have inventory on hand. (See **broker.**)

Debit Balance The amount of loan in a margin account.

Deficit A negative balance of trade or payments.

Delivery An FX trade where both sides make and take actual delivery of the currencies traded.

Depreciation A fall in the value of a currency due to market forces.

Derivative A generic term often applied to a wide variety of financial instruments that derive their cash flows, and therefore their value, by reference to an underlying asset, reference rate, or index.

Devaluation The deliberate downward adjustment of a currency's price, normally by official announcement.

Divergence Technical Analysis term used to describe a condition when prices and indicators fail to act in unison. Divergences present some of the best opportunities in trading.

E

Economic Indicator A government issued statistic that indicates current economic growth and stability. Common indicators include employment rates, gross domestic product (GDP), inflation, and retail sales.

Electronic Commerce Business that is transacted via the Internet, sometimes referred to as "e-commerce."

Electronic Communications Networks (ECNs) Electronic stock exchanges that facilitate the rapid executions of customer orders. Some ECNs can only execute an order when there is a similar internal order while others have a computer algorithm that allows their system to seek other means of filling the customers orders.

Eligibility Rules The Code of Arbitration states that no claim shall be eligible for submission to arbitration where six years have lapsed from the occurrence or event giving rise to the controversy.

Elliott Wave Theory A pattern-recognition technique published by Ralph Nelson Elliott in 1939 that believes all markets move in five distinct waves when traveling in the direction of a primary trend and three distinct waves when moving in a correction against a primary trend.

End of Day Order (EOD) An order to buy or sell at a specified price. This order remains open until the end of the trading day, which is typically 5 PM ET.

European Monetary Union (EMU) The principal goal of the EMU is to establish a single European currency called the euro, which officially replaced the national currencies of the member EU countries in 2002. On January 1, 1999 the transitional phase to introduce the euro began. The euro now exists as a banking currency and paper financial transactions and foreign exchanges are made in euros. This transition period will last for three years, at which time euro notes and coins will enter circulation. On July 1, 2002, euros became the only legal tender for EMU participants, and the national currencies of the member countries ceased to exist. The current members are Germany, France, Belgium, Luxembourg, Austria, Finland, Ireland, the Netherlands, Italy, Spain, and Portugal.

Euro The currency of the European Monetary Unit. A replacement for the European Currency Unit (ECU).

European Central Bank (ECB) The central bank for the new European Monetary Union.

Executive Sessions A private conference between the arbitrators during the course of the hearing to determine matters that have arisen such as evidentiary objections or motions.

Exhaustion Gap A gap in price that signals the end of a trend with one last burst of enthusiasm or fear.

F

Failure to Execute The failure of a broker to execute an order of his/her customer.

Fast Market A market condition in which a large number of orders are received within a short period of time. Orders arrive faster than the brokers-specialists and market makers can handle effectively. These situations are often caused by the announcement of some unexpected news.

Federal Reserve (Fed) The Central Bank for the United States.

Fibonacci (Fibs) Technical indicator based to the mathematical tendency of trends to find support at the 385%, 505%, or 62% retracement of the last major move.

Fill or Kill (FOK) An order that requires execution of the entire quantity immediately at the specified price. If not, the order is canceled.

Flat/Square Dealer lingo used to describe a position that has been completely reversed. For example, you bought $500,000 then sold $500,000, thereby creating a neutral (flat) position.

Foreign Exchange (Forex, FX)—the simultaneous buying of one currency and selling of another.

Filing Delivery to the director of arbitration of the statement of claim or other pleadings, to be kept on file as a matter of public record and reference.

Forward The prespecified exchange rate for a foreign exchange contract settling at some agreed future date based upon the interest rate differential between the two currencies involved.

Forward Points The pips added to or subtracted from the current exchange rate to calculate a forward price.

Fundamental Analysis Analysis of economic and political information with the objective of determining future movements in a financial market.

Futures Agreement to buy or sell a predetermined amount of a commodity or financial instrument at a certain price on a stipulated date.

Futures Contract Agreement to buy or sell a set number of shares of a specific stock in a designated future month at a price agreed upon by the buyer and seller. The contracts themselves are often traded on the futures market. A futures contract differs from an option because an option is the right to buy or sell, whereas a futures contract is the promise to actually make a transaction.

G

Generally Accepted Accounting Principles (GAAP) Rules, conventions, standards, and procedures that are widely accepted among financial accountants. Since 1973, GAAP doctrine has been established by the Financial Accounting Standards Board (FASB), an independent, self-regulating organization.

Good 'Til Cancelled Order (GTC) An order that does not expire until it is either executed or canceled. Some brokerages will cancel all GTC orders after 60 days. Make sure you check their rules and procedures first.

Guardian Someone authorized to manage the property of another who is incapable of managing the property themselves due to their age, lack of understanding or lack of self-control.

H

Hammer A candlestick reversal pattern that is formed when prices open up and sell off within the period and then rally to close near the open price. The pattern has a small body and a long wick below it.

Harami Term used to describe the position of a candlestick in which the open-close range is much smaller than the high-low range and sits within the real body of a tall prior bar.

Hedge To reduce the risk in one security by taking an offsetting position in a related security.

Held A situation where a security is temporarily not available for trading. Market makers are not allowed to display quotes of held securities.

Historical Volatility The range of price movement over an extended period of time as compared to current activity.

House Requirement The minimum amount of equity brokerage firms require margin clients to maintain in the account.

I

Individual Investor A person who buys or sells securities for his/her own account. The individual investor is also called a retail investor or retail shareholder.

Inflation The rate at which the general level of prices for goods and services is rising.

Initial Margin The initial deposit of collateral required to enter into a position as a guarantee on future performance.

Inside Day A price bar whose price range for the day is within that of the previous day. It has a lower high and higher low than the bar that preceded it.

Institutional Investor A bank, mutual fund, pension fund, or other corporate entity that trades securities in large volumes.

Interbank Rates The Foreign Exchange rates at which large international banks quote other large international banks.

Investor a person who buys or sells securities for his/her own account or the account of others. (See **Individual Investor.**)

J

Joint Account An account with two or more individuals acting as co-owners.

Joint Tenants With Rights of Survivorship (JTWROS) A joint account that allows the remaining tenant(s) to retain the deceased tenant's interest in the account.

L

Last Sale The price at which the security last traded.

Last Sale Service A service that allows real-time access to last-sale information reported by market makers.

Leading Indicators Statistics that are considered to predict future economic activity.

LIBOR The London Inter-Bank Offered Rate. Banks use LIBOR when borrowing from another bank.

Limit In relation to order instructions, the limit would specify the minimum selling or maximum buying price.

Limit Order An order to buy or sell a security at a customer-specified price; a customer order to buy or sell a specified number of shares of a security at a specified price.

Liquidation 1. Closing out a position. 2. An action taken by the margin department when a client hasn't paid for a purchase.

Liquidity The liquidity of a stock is the case with which the market can absorb volume buying or selling, without dramatic fluctuation in price.

Liquidity Ratio The liquidity of a stock is the ease with which the market can absorb volume buying or selling, without dramatic fluctuation in price.

Listed Securities Securities that trade on a national exchange.

Loan Consent Agreement An agreement whereby the customer gives the brokerage firm permission to lend his securities.

Loan Market Value The value of securities in a customers account.

Long Position A position that appreciates in value if market prices increase.

Low The lowest closing price of a stock over a certain period of time.

M

Margin An account in which a customer purchases securities on credit extended by a broker/dealer. It is the required equity that an investor must deposit to collateralize a position.

Margin Call A request from a broker or dealer for additional funds or other collateral to guarantee performance on a position that has moved against the customer.

Market Maker A firm that maintains a firm bid and offer price in a given security by standing ready to buy or sell at publicly quoted prices. The Nasdaq Stock Market is a decentralized network of competitive market makers. Market makers process orders for their own customers, and for other NASD broker/dealers; all NASD securities are traded through market maker firms. Market makers also will buy securities from issuers for resale to customers or other broker/dealers. About 10% of NASD firms are market makers (if the firm meets capitalization standards set down by NASD).

Market Maker Spread The difference between the price at which a market maker is willing to buy a security and the price at which the firm is willing to sell it.

Market Not Held A market order in which the floor trader has the discretion to execute the order when he/she feels it is best.

Market Order An order to buy or sell a stated amount of a security at the best possible price at the time the order is received in the marketplace.

Market Risk Exposure to changes in market prices.

Mark-to-Market Process of reevaluating all open positions with the current market prices. These new values then determine margin requirements.

Maturity The date for settlement or expiry of a financial instrument.

Minimum Maintenance Established by the exchanges' margin rules, the level to which the equity in an account may fall before the client must deposit additional equity. It is expressed as a percentage relationship between debit balance and equity or between market value and equity.

Moving Average Technical analysis tool that calculates the average price of a security or commodity over a period of time. This period can be as short as a few days or as long as several years.

N

Narrow Range Bar (NR) A price bar with a smaller range as compared to the prior bar's high-low range.

Narrowest Range of the Last 7 Bars (NR7) A low volatility time-price convergence that often precedes a major price expansion. A price bar with a smaller high-low range as compared to the prior six bars high-low range.

Neckline A trendline drawn under the support of a head and shoulders pattern or over the resistance of an inverse head and shoulders pattern.

Negotiable A feature of a security that enables the owner to transfer ownership or title.

Net Change The difference between today's last trade and the previous day's last trade.

Neutral One or more individuals assigned to mediate through negotiations or arbitrate by adjudication claims between or among disputing parties.

New Account Information Form Document filled out by a broker that details vital facts about a new client's financial circumstances and investment objectives.

Noise Price and volume fluctuations that confound the interpretation of market direction.

Not Held (NH) An order that gives discretion to the Floor broker as to time and price. The floor broker is "not held" responsible for capturing the best price.

O

Offer The rate at which a dealer is willing to sell a currency.

Offsetting Transaction A trade that serves to cancel or offset some or all of the market risk of a position.

On Balance Volume (OBV) A volume indicator that measures the amount of accumulation distribution occurring in a stock.

One Cancels the Other Order (OCO) A designation for two orders whereby one part of the two orders is executed the other is automatically canceled.

Open Order An order to buy or sell a security that remains in effect until it is either canceled by the customer or executed.

Open Position A deal not yet reversed or settled with a physical payment.

Order Ticket A form completed by a registered representative of a brokerage firm upon receiving order instructions from a customer.

OTC Bulletin Board An electronic service that provides selected quotes on over-the-counter stocks.

Over the Counter (OTC) Used to describe any transaction that is not conducted over an exchange.

Overbought The extremes of price movement to the upside where prices are likely to run out of buying pressures.

Overnight A trade that remains open until the next business day.

Oversold The extremes of price movement to the downside where prices are likely to run out of selling pressures.

P

Pattern Analysis Method of analyzing charts. Their objectives are to identify patterns that are formed in order to predict the future price direction.

Pennants Type of chart pattern.

Pips Digits added to or subtracted from the fourth decimal place, i.e. 0.0001. Also called points.

Political Risk Exposure to changes in governmental policy which will have an adverse effect on an investor's position.

Portfolio An individual's or institution's combined investment holdings. This includes cash, stocks, bonds, mutual funds, and real estate.

Position The netted total holdings of a given currency.

Premium In the currency market, describes the amount by which the forward or futures price exceed the spot price.

Previous Day's Close The previous day's last reported trade.

Price Transparency Describes quotes to which every market participant has equal access.

Program Trading Refers to trading done by large institutions that trade based on computer-generated signals. These orders are usually entered directly from the trader's computer to the market's computer system and executed automatically.

Q

Qualified Institutional Investor An institutional investor permitted under Securities and Exchange Commission rules to trade placed securities with other qualified institutional investors without registering the securities with the SEC. A qualified institutional investor must have at least $100 million under management.

Quote The highest bid and lowest offer on a given security at a particular time.

Quotation Size The maximum number of shares per order of a particular security that a market maker is willing to buy or sell at his/her current price.

R

Random Walk Classic theory that chaos drives all market activity and that price movement cannot be predicted.

Range The difference between the high and low trading price during a given period.

Rate The price of one currency in terms of another, typically used for dealing purposes.

Rectangle Small continuation pattern that points sideways to the primary trend.

Relative Strength Index A technical indicator invented by J. Welles Wilder that measures overbought, oversold, and divergent market situations.

Resistance Price level where selling pressures were strong enough to interrupt a price advance. Prices tend to these levels on the way up and reverse its direction.

Revaluation An increase in the exchange rate for a currency as a result of central bank intervention. Opposite of devaluation.

Reverse Head and Shoulders This classic reversal pattern forms from an extended low that sits between two higher lows. Three relative highs above the three lows connect at a trendline known as the neckline. Popular opinion expects a major rally when the neckline breaks.

Rising Wedge Reversal pattern that slowly rises in an uptrend until the price suddenly ejects into a sell-off.

Risk The inherent possibility that an investment will lose value.

Risk Management The employment of financial analysis and trading techniques to reduce and/or control exposure to various types of risk.

Roll-Over Process whereby the settlement of a deal is rolled forward to another value date. The cost of this process is based on the interest rate differential of the two currencies.

S

Settlement The process by which a trade is entered into the books and records the counterparts to a transaction. The settlement of currency trades may or may not involve the actual physical exchange of one currency for another.

Shooting Star A candlestick reversal pattern with a small real body, long wick (at least twice the length of the real body) above it, and a small or nonexistent tail below it.

Short Position An investment position that benefits from a decline in market price.

Spot Price The current market price. Settlement of spot transactions usually occurs within two business days.

Spread The difference between the bid and offer price.

Sterling Slang for British pound.

Stochastics Technical indicator in the oscillator class that was popularized by George Lane. It compares the relationship between the closing price and its price range over a given period of time.

Stop-Loss Order Order type whereby an open position is automatically liquidated at a specific price. Often used to minimize exposure to losses if the market moves against an investor's position.

Support Price levels where buying pressures were stronger than the selling pressures. Support levels interrupt a price decline and prices usually reverse and go up from there.

Symmetrical Triangle A chart pattern formed when price moves sideways, the highs are lower from peak to peak, and the lows are higher from trough to trough.

Swap A currency swap is the simultaneous sale and purchase of the same amount of a given currency at a forward exchange rate.

T

Technical Analysis Type of analysis that studies crowd behavior through price and volume activity. The intention is to predict future price movements.

Tomorrow Next Simultaneous buying and selling of a currency for delivery the following day.

Transaction Cost The cost of buying or selling a financial instrument.

Trade Date The date on which a trade occurs.

Trading Authorization Written permission for one to trade in another's account.

Trading Range The difference between the high and low prices traded during a period of time.

Trendline A line that connects a series of highs or lows. The slope of this line determines the direction of the trend. Trendlines also serve as support in an uptrend or resistance in a downtrend. Horizontal trendlines mark support resistance and range-bound conditions.

Triangles A type of chart pattern that looks like a triangle after the trendlines are drawn.

Turnover The total money value of all executed transactions in a given time period; volume.

Two-Way Price When both a bid and offer rate is quoted for a FX transaction.

U

Unauthorized Trading The purchase, sale, or trade of securities in an investor's account without the investor's prior authorization.

Uptick A transaction executed at a price higher than the preceding transaction in that security.

Uptick Rule In the United States, a regulation whereby a security may not be sold short unless the last trade prior to the short sale was at a price lower than the price at which the short sale is executed.

U.S. Prime Rate The interest rate at which U.S. banks will lend to their prime corporate customers.

Value Date The date on which counterparts to a financial transaction agree to settle their respective obligations, i.e., exchanging payments. For spot currency transactions, the value date is normally two business days forward. Also known as maturity date.

Variation Margin Funds a broker must request from the client to have the required margin deposited. The term usually refers to additional funds that must be deposited as a result of unfavorable price movements.

Volatility The degree of price fluctuation for a given asset, rate, or index. Usually expressed as a variance or standard deviation.

Volume Amount of trading activity, expressed in shares or dollars, experienced by a single security or the entire market within a specified period, usually daily, monthly, or annually.

W

When-Issued Trading A short form of "when, as, and if issued." The term refers to a conditional security: one authorized for issuance but not yet actually issued. All "when issued" transactions are on an "if" basis, to be settled if and when the actual security is issued.

Whipsaw Slang for a condition of a highly volatile market where a sharp price movement is quickly followed by a sharp reversal.

W-Type Bottom Another name for the double-bottom chart pattern.

Yard Slang for a billion.

About the CD-ROM

INTRODUCTION

This appendix provides you with information on the contents of the CD that accompanies this book. For the latest and greatest information, please refer to the ReadMe file located at the root of the CD.

SYSTEM REQUIREMENTS

- A computer with a processor running at 120 Mhz or faster
- At least 32 MB of total RAM installed on your computer; for best performance, we recommend at least 64 MB
- A CD-ROM drive

USING THE CD-ROM WITH WINDOWS

To install the items from the CD to your hard drive, follow these steps:

1. Insert the CD into your computer's CD-ROM drive.
2. The CD-ROM interface will appear. The interface provides a simple point-and-click way to explore the contents of the CD.

If the opening screen of the CD-ROM does not appear automatically, follow these steps to access the CD:

1. Click the Start button on the left end of the taskbar and then choose Run from the menu that pops up.
2. In the dialog box that appears, type *d:* **Start.exe.** (If your CD-ROM drive is not drive d, fill in the appropriate letter in place of *d*.) This brings up the CD Interface described in the preceding set of steps.

USING THE CD WITH MAX OS X

To install the items from the CD to your hard drive, follow these steps:

1. Insert the CD into your computer's CD-ROM drive.
2. Click on the **StartHere.html** file to view the media content on the CD.
3. To install software browse to the software folder and click on the installer icon.

WHAT'S ON THE CD

The following sections provide a summary of the software and other materials you'll find on the CD.

CONTENT

Any material from the book, including forms, slides, and lesson plans if available, are in the folder named "Media". To view the files use the interface provided.

APPLICATIONS

The following application is on the CD:

Macromedia Flash Player

Flash Player is a freeware application for viewing multimedia Flash files.

Shareware programs are fully functional, trial versions of copyrighted programs. If you like particular programs, register with their authors for a nominal fee and receive licenses, enhanced versions, and technical support.

Freeware programs are copyrighted games, applications, and utilities that are free for personal use. Unlike shareware, these programs do not require a fee or provide technical support.

GNU software is governed by its own license, which is included inside the folder of the GNU product. See the GNU license for more details.

Trial, demo, or evaluation versions are usually limited either by time or functionality (such as being unable to save projects). Some trial versions are very sensitive to system date changes. If you alter your computer's date, the programs will "time out" and no longer be functional.

CUSTOMER CARE

If you have trouble with the CD-ROM, please call the Wiley Product Technical Support phone number at (800) 762-2974. Outside the United States, call 1(317) 572-3994. You can also contact Wiley Product Technical Support at *http://www.wiley.com/techsupport*. John Wiley & Sons will provide technical support only for installation and other general quality control items. For technical support on the applications themselves, consult the program's vendor or author.

To place additional orders or to request information about other Wiley products, please call (877) 762-2974.

Index

Register At www.raghee.com/5free and receive

Five FREE Invaluable Trading Tools

- 100% REBATE OF YOUR BOOK PURCHASE
  (Some restrictions apply)
- DEMO TRADING ACCOUNT WITH FXCM
- NEWSLETTER DIRECT FROM RAGHEE
- SPECIAL FREE OFFER FROM eSIGNAL
- TRIALS OF THE BEST TRADING TOOLS
  www.raghee.com

FOUR WAYS TO REGISTER:

1: GO TO www.raghee.com/5free

2: FILL IN THE POST CARD BELOW AND DROP IT IN THE MAIL

3: CALL (877) 864-3727 AND TELL THE OPERATOR YOU WANT TO REGISTER
   FOR Raghee's 5-free DEAL!!!

4: FILL IN THE POST CARD BELOW AND FAX TO: (818) 789-0979

The last option is
*   do nothing,*
*   get nothing, and*
*   achieve nothing...*

"FIVE FREE" REGISTRATION FORM

Name _____

Address _____

City _____ State ____ Zip _____

Day Phone _____ Evening Phone _____

E-Mail _____

DO YOU CURRENTLY TRADE
What Markets   ☐ ForeX   ☐ Stocks   ☐ Futures
☐ OTHER _____

Website: www.raghee.com • E-Mail: info@raghee.com • Fax: (818) 789-0979 • Phone: 877-864-3727

Superior Management, LLC,
DBA In Touch
P.O. Box 261460,
Encino, Ca 91426